SHADOWMASTER

The vile curse of Chaos stalks the wild lands of northern Allansia. Cruel bandits raid the villages, killing and looting as they go. Everyone, it seems, is powerless to stop them. Now, though, the attackers are in search of a treasure far more valuable than gold. Driven by their inhuman leader, they are in pursuit of the key that will unlock the very mysteries of life and death itself!

The sorcerer Yaztromo, for so long the self-appointed guardian of the lands around Darkwood Forest, cannot stand idly by while his countrymen are put to the sword. With Chadda Darkmane, newly returned from defeating the demon Rivel, close at hand, the wizard embarks on a quest to discover the source of the raids and the real reason behind them.

What they discover is that when Chaos has dominion, nothing can ever be as it seems. Fair hides foul, insanity hides inner order, and darkness lurks deep within the light. Can Yaztromo and Darkmane defeat all these illusions to discover the real master of the shadows? Only *Shadowmaster*, the third Fighting Fantasy novel following *The Trolltooth Wars* and *Demonstealer*, can tell you!

Ian Livingstone with Steve Jackson created the hugely successful Fighting Fantasy series and are co-founders of Games Workshop Ltd. Marc Gascoigne, the Fighting Fantasy consultant editor, is the author of *Demonstealer*, *Out of the Pit*, *Titan* and *Battleblade Warrior*, and co-author of *Dungeoneer* and *Blacksand*.

Ian Livingstone
with
Marc Gascoigne

SHADOWMASTER

Illustrated by Russ Nicholson

PUFFIN BOOKS

PUFFIN BOOKS

Published by the Penguin Group
Penguin Books Ltd, 27 Wrights Lane, London w8 5tz, England
Penguin Books USA Inc., 375 Hudson Street, New York, New York 10014, USA
Penguin Books Australia Ltd, Ringwood, Victoria, Australia
Penguin Books Canada Ltd, 10 Alcorn Avenue, Toronto, Ontario, Canada m4v 3b2
Penguin Books (NZ) Ltd, 182–190 Wairau Road, Auckland 10, New Zealand

Penguin Books Ltd, Registered Offices: Harmondsworth, Middlesex, England

First published 1992
1 3 5 7 9 10 8 6 4 2

Concept copyright © Steve Jackson and Ian Livingstone, 1992
Text copyright © Ian Livingstone with Marc Gascoigne, 1992
Illustrations copyright © Russ Nicholson, 1992
All rights reserved

The moral right of the author has been asserted

Printed in England by Clays Ltd, St Ives plc
Filmset in 11/12 Monophoto Palatino

This book is for Bill King,
the real Master of Shadows.

Contents

Shadowmaster

1

The Fourth Village

With a noise like the rustling shrouds of a horde of hungry ghosts, the next sheaf of arrows rained down from the sky. Whether by chance or design, one caught the woman standing directly next to the village chieftain, pinning her to the door by her neck, and she hung there, eyes frozen in surprise, a scream of terror left forever half formed on her lips, her axe slipping gently from limp fingers. Feeling rather than seeing the space beside him, the chieftain glanced around but barely had time to acknowledge his cohort's death before something far more pressing took his full attention. Squat shapes were running in front of the blazing ruin of the village alehouse, dark shadows readying swords and clubs in anticipation of the savage battle to come.

'Get ready! Here they come again!' the chieftain called out in his deep, rounded voice. Earlier his warning would have caused his fellow defenders to jump into action without a second thought, but now he could hear his words dissipate on the breeze, lost among the cries of the wounded and the crackling of the flames from the burning buildings. He felt the sense of dread grow

11

perceptibly and fought to calm his rising panic. He was their chieftain, and fear of defeat was not a quality to be found in a chieftain.

'Choose your target, and make every blow count,' he muttered, more to reassure himself than to be heard by the men and women around him. He hefted his sword in his large, leathery hands, accustoming himself to its weight, his fingers matching every indentation in the leather-bound grip exactly. By day the man was Old-castle's blacksmith; he was still wearing the leather apron indicative of his trade, although, when the alarm was raised an hour previously, he had managed to tug a breastplate over his chest and jam his battered old helmet down on top of his wayward mane of nut-brown hair. 'For Oldcastle! For your children!' came the chief-tain's battle-cry, and the onslaught began once more.

The attackers had come out of the forest from several directions. Their horsemen leapt over the bodies of the gatekeepers who had been picked off, scant seconds before, by the arrows of unseen archers; they were closely followed by a scuttling force of inhumans of various races. Despite their ragged armour and weap-onry, the raiders were plainly well disciplined. Within moments they had taken control of the main gate of the village and defeated the first line of defence in a single easy swoop. Chief Norska Val, hammering a horseshoe into shape round his anvil, at first had not heard the cries coming from the gate but, when he saw the feet of the fleeing traders scurrying by, he had reacted quickly. As he ran from his workshop, tightening the last strap on his breastplate, he grabbed the arm of the first person to pass him. The daughter of Waelun the miller had given a startled shriek but calmed enough to listen to his command to her to run and ring the warning bell, located in the keep for just such an eventuality.

The bell was sounding its sonorous note across the village as Val reached the marketplace, near the gate. The stallholders closest to the gate had been unable to escape and were now defending themselves against the attackers as best they could. Someone had remained calm enough to overturn a number of stalls in order to create a makeshift barricade; it had held up the raiders' advance for a while, as if they had not been expecting even this token resistance. Now, however, several Orcs and Goblins had broken through and were battling their way through the mêlée of untrained villagers. The chieftain had taken the first of the raiders in the chest with his sword, the shock of the impact making his huge frame rattle. As the Orc collapsed in the dirt, Val was startled to see from its blue eyes and human-proportioned facial features that it was a half-breed.

As he engaged his second opponent, he heard the familiar rumbling voice of Oldcastle's alehouse keeper, Cormis Redhair, ordering the villagers to fall back as far as his property, where his sons and daughters were erecting a stronger barricade and marshalling their forces. Redhair was a soldier of fortune, now long retired – but plainly, he still knew a thing or two about battle. Norska Val slashed with his sword, sending a short, wart-studded Lizard Man-like warrior crashing backwards, its innards spilling out through a gaping wound in its leathery hide; he ran to join Redhair and the villagers.

Since that first attack, the battle had gone from bad to worse, and thence to desperate. The makeshift barricade – several carriages piled with empty barrels and planks scavenged from the nearest market-stalls – had hardly been strong enough to remain standing by itself, let alone to repulse the bandits. The ramshackle force swept through the ruined marketplace, hacking down human stragglers without mercy. They were led by several brutish Trolls and Orcs mounted on mad-eyed horses so starved that their skins appeared translucent. They leapt the barricade with ease and crashed down among the milling villagers so that their riders could slash haphazardly at the poorly protected defenders. Val himself had accounted for a couple of riders before the foot troops who were scrambling over the upturned carts forced him to turn his attention to them instead.

Some of the raiders who were not in the vanguard of the attack veered to the left and right and spread out through the village. A short but bloody battle was fought inside the alehouse itself, as Redhair's ex-adventuress wife and two of their sons duelled with at least seven opponents before they made their escape, locking and barring the only door then retreating towards the relative safety of the crumbling stone keep which gave Oldcastle its name.

Now the battle was surely increasing in intensity, in readiness for its final phase. Equal numbers of warriors contested on each side, plus twice as many human children and the elderly; but it was plain that the bandits had the advantage of better training and discipline and they carried finer weapons. Many of the villagers had had no formal training in warfare and were armed with nothing better than pitchforks or carving knives. Some of the village's wooden houses were ablaze, as were the thatched roofs of a few of the older buildings. The villagers had retreated as far as they were physically able, their backs now against the overgrown walls of the keep. As all the able men and women readied themselves for the final clash, the children and old folk hurried inside to take advantage of what little protection the old fortification provided.

Several centuries previously, the building of the ancient stronghold had been started in order to provide the centrepiece for a large castle complex. Before it was half-way finished, however, its nobleman owner and his people had all been put to the sword by a rival prince, and the work was abandoned. Now, all that remained was the central hall, a few smaller ground-floor rooms and a number of half-finished underground chambers. Above ground-floor level, a number of shattered towers enclosing the remains of spiral staircases rose a short distance. The whole ruin looked like the bony skeleton of a proper castle that has been stripped of its stony outer flesh. It would not hold out for long against such a determined assault.

Stepping lightly over the body of one of the gatekeepers who was sprawled, face down, in the mud, the commander of the bandits entered the village. A thin smile playing on his gaunt face, he strode in leisurely fashion through the ruined marketplace, noting without perceptible emotion the bodies – a few bandits, many humans – scattered around. Ahead of him came the shouts of human and inhuman alike as they prepared for the next attack; but the commander no more heard them than he noted either the groans of the injured scattered all round him, the crackling of the flames from the blazing alehouse or the creak of his ancient leather armour. The smoke from the alehouse fire enveloped him for a few seconds, flowing round him as a cloud shapes itself to a mountain. When he emerged at the far side, he paused for a while, waiting for his second-in-command to observe his presence and report to him on the progress of their mission. He did not have long to wait.

More arrows flew in an arc from behind the front line of advancing bandits. The smoke from the burning buildings was blowing into the faces of the human defenders, making it almost impossible to see the missiles as they plummeted down into the crowd of villagers lined up between the two crumbling walls which were all that remained of the ruined keep's old guardhouses. Several of the black-feathered arrows hit home and people fell, wounded. Other villagers stepped forward to fill some of the gaps, but in others a space remained.

Screaming a challenge, the front rows of defenders, led by Norska Val and Cormis Redhair, ran forward to meet the advancing enemy. Pandemonium broke out once more, the stifling, smoke-filled air ringing with the clash of steel and the shouts and screams of human and inhuman warriors.

Here, a furry-pelted Orc-creature swung an immense, iron-bound mace wildly over its head, screaming with delighted blood-lust the same words, over and over and over again, as it sent its terrified opponents flying: 'Hoo-man – drop dead, drop dead! Huh-hur!' There, a woman usually to be found repairing cartwheels darted beneath the arm of a Lizard Man-like bandit and stuck her shortsword into its unprotected lower quarters. With a triumphant yelp, she spun and was quick enough then to slice deep into the arm of a chattering Goblin-thing. Distracted, the creature turned its head as if offering its neck to its other opponent, one of Redhair's sons. He did not waste the opportunity: his sword struck home with tremendous force. The woman staggered back, rubbing her eyes to clear her vision, queasy with the sudden realization of what she had just done. Redhair's son grabbed her arm, wiped his other sleeve across her face and stared hard into her frightened eyes. 'Time to panic is over, Olena. Follow me now!' he commanded and ran to rejoin the fray. Without a second thought, the woman followed, readying her weapon once more.

Val and Redhair were side by side, in the very middle of the fighting. Between them they had accounted for half a dozen raiders, from stunted Goblins to a towering, Troll-like creature with a lizard's head. The air around them positively sang with the passage of their sword and battle-axe. The sweat poured from them and they were covered in small cuts and bruises; although their task was grim, they were both grinning as if sharing a private joke rather than fighting for their own lives and those of their people. In times long past, both had made their living by the sword, and now they discovered with delight that neither had lost his instinctive feel for battle.

But it was clear that, for all their skill, they could not hold out alone against the overwhelming attack of the bandits. Redhair had trained his sons and daughters in the ways of combat, and all were acquitting themselves bravely – but all around their untrained neighbours were falling to their savage opponents. Now when a villager fell there was no one to step into his or her place. The bandits were beginning to regroup in order to kill the remaining humans, picking them off like so many pigs in a pen.

Val finished off his Orc opponent with a final stab of his swordpoint and glanced around to make an assessment of the situation. It was dire, and retreat was the only option. At his side, Redhair was struggling to defend himself against the ferocious blows of two opponents. While he engaged one Goblin-like creature with his axe, a slavering Lizard Man ran forward and stabbed under his guard with a short javelin. Alongside this battle, Redhair's daughter Yarna was holding her own against a tattoo-covered Orc. Before Val could get at Redhair's javelin-wielding opponent, the Lizard Man found a gap in the human's armour and thrust his weapon into his ribs. Redhair staggered back in shock as a wild slicing lunge from the Goblin opened his arm from elbow to wrist. Redhair dropped his axe, the leather thong round his other wrist keeping it from falling from him altogether, and staggered back with a howl that was a mixture of pain and anger.

Val grasped his old friend's shoulder and dragged him back to the rear of the turmoil. 'Retreat, Oldcastle, retreat!' he boomed, his words half lost beneath the continuing clamour of battle. Enough had heard him, though, to start fighting on the retreat towards the doors of the keep; their movements told their fellows what was happening. The rest of the villagers disengaged or finished off their enemies and fell back. As she turned to run, Redhair's daughter was dropped by a cruel blow from the tattooed Orc's mace which caught her square on the side of the head. She sprawled at the creature's feet, her blood staining the dirt a dark crimson.

The doors to the keep were made of sturdy hardwood, studded and bound with iron. It was with their backs to these doors that the human defenders of Oldcastle made their final stand. With Norska Val at their centre, they arranged themselves in a semi-circle, weapons jutting out like the quills of a porcupine. Most were injured, some seriously, others superficially, and all were exhausted beyond imagination; but now the final reckoning was upon them and they all knew they would gladly give their lives in defence of their village.

The Fourth Village

The bandits drew near, each hunched in a fighting stance, weapon thrust forward at the ready. Many were smiling, certain of the final outcome even before it took place. Except for the jingling and scraping of their armour and equipment, however, they made no sound. In the background, the crackling of flames and aching moans of the wounded could be heard plainly enough, but a dread silence had fallen over the empty ground which lay between the two sides.

A voice spoke. 'I think that is enough, don't you?' The voice was quiet and cultured, radiating unquenchable calm. The advancing line of raiders parted and their commander, until this moment hidden from the villagers, stepped forward. He was tall and hollow-cheeked; his old leather armour had been patched and re-patched, with repair piled on repair, until one could not tell whether anything remained of the original. At his belt hung a long, thin sword; one gloved hand rested upon its pommel as he walked. He was very pale-skinned, the stark whiteness of his youthful face contrasting with his dull black hair, which hung strangely long on one side of his head and short on the other. He came to a halt at the head of his troops and dropped his head a little by way of greeting.

Nonplussed, the villagers just stared.

'Now then, good people of Oldcastle, I don't think this affair need go any further, do you? We don't want to cause you any more trouble. We desire the contents of your treasury, so, if you will hand it over to us with good grace, we will leave you in peace. What do you say, eh?' He spoke calmly, a slight smile turning on his lips, but there was something in his voice, a mocking tone, that implied that he would be quick to anger should he not receive the expected response.

Shadowmaster

The burly blacksmith stepped forward and pulled himself to his full height. 'I am Norska Val, chief of these people.' The bandit commander nodded his head curtly, though whether out of respect or in mockery it was difficult to tell. 'We are far from defeated, and we shall make your men pay dearly for their attack upon us, before we shall be. We are not people to roll over like dogs and lie still while you butcher us. Begone, and take your ill-formed rabble with you.'

He was answered by the soft clapping of the commander's gloved hands. 'Bravo, Norska Val. I admire your courage, if not your common sense. I must assure you that we really do want just your riches, such as they may be. Since it is possible that you have raised the alarm and alerted the whole countryside to our presence here, I must insist that you hand it over forthwith, so that we may take our leave of you.' Val stood, stony-faced, in defiance. 'Very well,' the commander continued. 'What do you say to our wrestling for it?'

The villagers had not expected anything like this; many gasped, some even smiled wryly. Val was a huge bear of a man with limbs like the branches of an ancient tree, his muscles hardened by years at the forge; he would snap the sapling-thin bandit commander like a dry twig.

Val, too, was disconcerted. 'A trick! I make no deals with bandits. We lay down our arms ... and we are slaughtered where we stand.'

'I can assure you, Norska Val, that I am a creature of honour,' the commander replied, unruffled. He reached for his belt, unbuckled his scabbard and tossed it back to his second-in-command, a burly Troll. 'Come now; you against me, no complications. The winner takes the contents of your treasury and nothing more. Upon my

20

honour as a gentleman, sir, your people are safe. You win, and my men will leave, I guarantee it.'

Plainly Val was uncertain, but his people were not. 'Do it, Val. You'll tear him limb from limb. We have no choice, we have lost. You'll pull him apart. Grind his face in the dirt!'

The bandit leader smiled again. 'It seems the matter has been decided. Upon my honour, I swear that, if I win, we shall merely avail ourselves of your treasure and then depart as rapidly as we arrived. Now, shall we begin?' The commander stepped forward into the no-man's land between them, pulling his gloves off. Val made up his mind, though in truth his hand had already been forced. He too stepped forward, tossing his sword and helmet behind him.

'Would you mind if I take this off?' the commander said, gesturing at his chest.

'Bare-chested is how we wrestle here,' Val replied gruffly, pulling his jerkin over his head. He stood naked to the waist, his immense shoulders and chest rippling with sweat-sheened muscle. 'You take off what you want, bandit.'

The commander nodded again, the thin smile once more upon his lips. He turned his back to the chieftain and tugged at the buckles of his armoured jacket. It slipped from his shoulders, followed by his black shirt. The commander's skin now revealed was a peculiar mottled colour, covered with blotches the size of a lizard's scales. With a guttural howl, he suddenly leaned forward, as if taken ill, and a row of spines burst through the skin along his rippling back. He turned, his head elongating into a lizard-like snout and his mottled skin taking on a greenish hue. Hissing in delight, the Shapechanger completed his transformation: a three-pronged forked tongue flickered between long jaws and a spine-tipped tail flicked behind him.

'Now, Norska Val, let us wrestle!' The village chieftain knew he had been tricked but he could not now refuse the challenge. With a roar like distant thunder he leapt at the spiny creature. The Shapechanger spun and twisted under one questing arm and slashed upwards with a claw-edged hand. Four parallel cuts raked across Val's belly and blood fountained across the muddy ground. The human growled in agony and grasped the Shapechanger in a crushing bear-hug. The lizard-like being was lifted bodily off the ground, Norska Val's immense arms circling round his chest and back, squeezing, constricting, crushing. There was a sound like the snapping of a branch as a bone was broken by the human's overwhelming grip. The Shapechanger shrieked, a throaty yell that echoed round the makeshift arena.

Lifting his opponent with both hands, Val tensed his muscles again and applied still more pressure to the creature's spine. As the muscles in his arms swelled, he grinned in triumph. Then a pair of clawed hands grasped the sides of his head, distorting his mouth into a jagged scar. The Shapechanger lowered his fang-filled mouth and bit deeply into Val's forehead, and his skull splintered. The chieftain's arms slipped from round the creature's spiny body. Holding the limp body of the human upright with both hands, the Shapechanger chewed down with a disgusting, slurping noise.

Slowly, the creature let Val's head slip from between his hands, and it slumped in the mud. 'Gentleman,' he smiled wetly, 'I believe the treasure is ours. Round up all the villagers and disarm them. Do not harm a single one of them, or you will answer to me for it. Now hurry, for we must be gone from here.' The bandits ran to do his bidding.

The Fourth Village

Drifting in his world of quicksand memory and mist-swirl future, Axion watches all. Waiting, as he has always waited, in a dream of death and dust.

2

From a Distance

The old spiral staircase that wound up through the middle of the tower was in dire need of repair: many of the steps were rotten with woodworm, and some had collapsed altogether; but the old man who grunted his way slowly up them knew without looking which ones could still bear his not inconsiderable weight. With one hand on the rust-spotted iron rail and the other keeping the loose vermilion-and-blue robes away from his slippered feet, he climbed to the top. One day, he thought to himself, I really must hire a carpenter from one of the nearby villages to repair this confounded staircase. Then he chortled to himself, strangely happy with the knowledge that he would probably never get around to it. 'You're nothing but an idle old goat,' he chuckled out loud.

The stairs ended at a heavy oak door. The old man pushed it open and hesitated for a moment: the sudden light dazzled his eyes; the sun was shining directly in through the window which stood, half open, awaiting the return of his scout. Tiny motes of dust danced lazily in the golden glow, and the room was suffused with the comforting scent of warm books. The room ran the full width of the tower and every spare millimetre of space was crammed with shelves that were piled high with books and scrolls. More were piled on the desk, on the carved-wood high-backed chair which sat behind it, and on the faded rugs which covered the entire floor.

Through the open window, the old sorcerer could just make out the swaying tops of the nearest trees. The tower, which stood among the trees at the southern tip of the sprawling expanse of woodland known as Darkwood Forest, had been his home for nearly forty years. Why he had chosen to live so near this sinister forest was something of a mystery to most of the folk who knew of him; it was well known that Darkwood was the lair of some of the most evil creatures in all Allansia. Some explained it away by saying that Yaztromo's magic was so powerful that he had no reason to fear any living creature. Others, less kind, put it down to his desire to behave like a hermit, a miserable recluse who hid away from normal people.

The truth of the matter was a combination of both theories. His magic was indeed very powerful, though this was partly because of where his tower was located; but he certainly also preferred the peace and quiet of his isolated tower to the prattling gossip of the village and its inhabitants, who did not understand his ways. This preference went double so far as his friends in the Dwarfish settlements were concerned – but, then, Dwarfs could quite happily spend hours gossiping about any-body they considered strange – and that meant just about anybody who, not being a Dwarf, failed to follow the traditional Dwarfish customs. Nevertheless, despite that, Yaztromo loved them because all of them to a man – and to a woman, for that matter – had their heart in the right place. Whenever danger threatened, the Dwarfs were always ready to pick up their crossbows and war-

25

hammers to defend not just their own lands but also those around them. Evil, they said often enough, had to be defeated, no matter where it took hold. Hmm, that reminded him: he would ask the Dwarfs if they could take a look at his staircase when they came to repair the tower's glass dome that had been damaged in a fire a few months previously.

The old wizard walked round his desk and put one hand up to shade his ancient eyes and stare out eastwards. 'Why is it,' he muttered in irritation, 'that crows are so damned unreliable? Where is that confounded bird? If he had been a chicken, I swear I would have had him served up on a dinner plate long before now, for all the use he is to me. I want news!'

'Yaaaz! Yaaaz!' came a sudden squawk from above. As Yaztromo spun around, a sleek, jet-black crow swept down, to land on the windowsill. It flapped its black wings a few times before folding them carefully behind its shiny breast and stood motionless, staring at the old man with what could easily be taken for a cheeky grin running the length of its long yellow beak.

'I told you not to call me that!' said the old wizard, a stern look fixed on that small part of his face which was not hidden by silvery-white hair. 'My name is Yaztromo, spelt Y-A-Z-T-R-O-M-O! How many times must I tell you? Do you understand — or do you wish to give up the power of speech, my little flying friend?'

'R-r-roark! R-r-roark! You wouldn't threaten a harmless, craawwk, woodland creature, would you, Yaaaz?'

'Oh, I give up! Vermithrax, you're the worst pet a wizard would ever

dread to have,' the old man said with a sigh, shaking his head. 'Now tell me what you saw. What causes that plume of smoke? Is it what I feared?'

'Worse,' came the squawked reply. 'Village you call Oldcastle was burning, as you said. R-roark! No accident, though, that cause the fire. Yaaaz, village was under attack!'

The wizard's hand, that had been stroking his beard, stopped, and he fixed the crow with a steely gaze. 'Attack, you say? Who would attack Oldcastle? No, you don't need to tell me. Bandits – again!' He thumped his fist on the desk, sending a tiny spray of gold-green sparks shimmering up his wrist.

Vermithrax flapped his wings in agreement. 'True as I eat worms, Yaaaz! Nasty Orcy bandits, on foot and horses too. Burnt the village, r-roark, killed many people.'

'I knew it!' Yaztromo ran his fingers distractedly through his tangled white mane of hair. 'Did you manage to follow them? Which way did they go?'

'Sunrise, into the Moonstones, just like last time. Crawk! Must be same lot!' Vermithrax hopped from one foot to the other and gestured with one wing across the room, towards the east.

'I hate to tell you this, you scraggy bag of feathers, but I fear you are right.' Yaztromo sat down at his desk, then reached over to the pile of scrolls lying next to his chair. Finding the one he needed, he sat back up straight with a creak of old bones. Unrolled, it proved to be a crudely drawn chart mapping the land between Dark-wood and the Moonstone Hills to the east.

'Now let me see . . . hmm – ah! here we are.' He tapped the small sketch of a tower near the southernmost end of the forest, then his finger glided across to the opposite side of the chart. 'The first raids were on caravans crossing the Moonstones, and on those two tiny shepherds' villages, in this area.' His finger inscribed a vague circle deep in that part of the map that was labelled Moonstone Hills. On the sill, Vermithrax craned his neck to peer over the wizard's shoulder. 'All those events took place months ago, before our young visitor left. The first big one was their raid on Tegris, down here along the bank of the Silver River. Old Stillbird of Tegris always was a cantankerous old so-and-so,' he muttered in an aside, and the crow gave him a look that bordered on the sarcastic. 'Everyone thought he had overstepped the mark in some matter of honour and that one of his neighbours had taught him a lesson he'd been needing for years.

'Trouble is, a few days later Oakwall was put to the torch too.' Yaztromo tapped an unmarked spot some distance to the north. 'One you can put down to territory, feuding clansmen, whatever. It seems to be what humans do to pass the time, make each other's lives a misery; never could see the point of it myself. We knew that wasn't the true story when . . .'

'C-crawwk! Kierdale! Nasty Goberlings burnt Kierdale! R-roark!' Vermithrax flapped his wings excitedly, craning his head to look at his tail where new feathers had only recently grown back.

'Kierdale, exactly; where a certain semi-evolved lizard nearly provided dinner for a sharp-shooting bandit because he disobeyed my orders and got far too close.' The crow hung its head in a vain attempt to look sheepish. 'However, you did manage to find out more about them: how many there were, what manner of creatures, and what they were after. And you say these were the same bandits?'

Vermithrax nodded vigorously. 'Smoke was thick so couldn't see fighting too well, r-roark, but looked the same as other time.'

Shadowmaster

'Many injured, you said? Hmm. Their chieftain, Norska
Val, has been a friend of mine ever since he was a hot-
headed young thing gallivanting around the countryside
and getting into terrible scrapes. I always said I would
pay him a visit when he was settled in; now, I think, the
time is somewhat overdue.'

The white-haired sorcerer started pacing the room,
sorting ideas out in his mind, barely aware that he was still
muttering out loud. 'Too many raids now. Even if they are
only after treasure, they are causing too much damage
pursuing it. I will not have it, not in my homeland!' He
paused. 'Listen to yourself, you senile old goat! Anyone
would think you ruled Allansia, the way you carry on. Yet I
have sworn to help protect this land in any way I can. And
there is nothing to be lost by finding out more about these
bandits.' Yaztromo looked up at his pet. 'Right, you rat-
with-wings. It is a two-day walk to Oldcastle, so you can
come with me and keep me company on my journey. But I
warn you! Any more cheekiness and I'll sell you to the first
merchant I meet and, before you know it, you'll be propping
up the crust on a pie at one of King Salamon's banquets!'

'R-roark!' Vermithrax replied.

Several hours later, a hunched figure emerged through
the door at the base of the tower. It was clad in a long,
grey, weatherproof robe and was carrying a straight,
sturdy staff; a small knapsack was thrown over one
shoulder. As Yaztromo said the words which would
magically lock his home against intruders until his return,
Vermithrax flapped down to perch on his shoulder. The
old sorcerer shot the bird a disgruntled look, then sighed
resignedly and turned to go. The setting sun made his
shadow stretch out ahead of him as he set off along the
narrow path that led through the trees.

3

Footsteps

Eight days earlier.

There they went again. Soft and careful, for sure, but neither soft enough nor careful enough to be hidden beneath the sound of Chadda Darkmane's own footsteps. He himself did not care how loud a noise he made; the cobblestones were wet and muddy from recent rain, but this slippery covering did little to muffle the sharp sound of the nails in his boots striking the ground sharply with every step.

Walking of any kind was proving somewhat trouble-some at the moment, since his body had not yet fully adapted to being on solid ground again. That part of his brain which controlled his balance continued to insist that he was still standing on a ship's violently pitching and rolling deck as each successive wave struck her bows. The fact that he was now trying to stride purpose-fully up Clog Street, the narrow lane leading from the harbour where he had disembarked over half an hour previously, was something his body was still trying manfully to come to terms with. Darkmane had enough control over his reflexes not to stagger up the street as if drunk; but every few paces his sense of balance would make him want to counteract the effect of another non-existent wave, and he would have to clamp down hard with his mind to stop his muscles from following suit.

He could be forgiven, perhaps, for imagining that he was still aboard ship. The lane rose and fell sharply, twisting and yawing as if its cobblestones were laid on top of a rough swell. The warm night air was full of the scent of the sea, a subtle distillation of a hundred smells, from the salty freshness blown by the breeze to the rank stench of decaying fish rotting on the quayside. Here in Clog Street, though, a new odour joined the others, wafting through, thick and dark; it told of hate and fear and of lies piled on lies and, above all, of the sweet decay of absolute corruption.

It was the stink of Port Blacksand, the City of Thieves. And at this very moment, three of its finest were stalking Chadda Darkmane through the shadow-choked streets.

At this time of the morning, perhaps three hours past the midnight bell, any other town or city would be deathly quiet, its good people sleeping safely in their beds, their rest undisturbed by the occasional footsteps of a patrolling city guardsman. Here in Blacksand, things were different. The scurvy knaves who comprised the City Guard and who were meant to be patrolling this district of the city-state were brawling noisily in the gutter outside the two rival quayside taverns, the Vulgar Goblin and the Hemlock, after a dispute as to which served the better – or perhaps the less bad – ale. Under strict and potentially fatal rules laid down by the city-state's fanatical ruler, Lord Azzur, the guardsmen were barred from using weapons to settle their domestic disputes – but, when several of one's opponents are

Footsteps

immense Trolls with fists the size of watermelons, a fight can quickly become very serious – indeed, life-threatening. Still, their brawling had allowed Darkmane to slip past them without a second glance, and this was a good omen. After spending three weeks at sea on a two-week voyage, he was in no mood for further delays.

The harbour-master, ever eager to swindle as much as he could from a new arrival, had discovered this too late. As the *Tempest Dancer* pulled into port, Eril Gor had come aboard from a small rowing-boat, ostensibly to assist in navigating the ship between the other vessels which lay at anchor in the harbour. His mind, as usual, was on other matters – profitable matters. His opening speech was well known to all who regularly served on the *Tempest Dancer*, or on any vessel which set down regularly at Blacksand, for that matter.

'As you know well, Captain Terrai,' Gor said as soon as he got aboard, 'no amount of gold or silver can persuade me to allow goods into or out of this city without the proper duty being paid.' Terrai did know this very well, for she had been running all manner of goods up and down the Pirate Coast for the best part of twelve years. As soon as her ship had rounded the last kink in the coast and had come in sight of the sprawling, corpse-like shadow that, from the sea, was Port Blacksand, she had sent two men below to divide up the cargo, separating a small portion and setting it aside for Gor. It rankled her that Gor demanded a rake-off in tradable goods, but a deal with him worked out far cheaper than paying duty at the official rate. In any case, this time she had other matters on her mind, as the fresh scar on her cheek attested.

Ten days into the final leg of the voyage, hopping up the coast from Arantis via Halak and Rimon, Terrai had decided to take advantage of the rough seas to indulge in a little personal piracy. Accompanied by her immense bos'n and an equally large mate, equipped with three razor-edged cutlasses, she had burst into Darkmane's cabin in the middle of the night with the intention of relieving him of his possessions. He had a choice, she told him simply: hand over his valuables and live or swim for the distant shore. Darkmane pointed out a third option, one that Terrai and her thugs had never encountered before.

Next morning the ship had a new, hurriedly promoted bos'n and its captain was wearing an unpleasant duelling-cut on her face. Darkmane was not directly troubled again for the remainder of the voyage, though the icy atmosphere which followed him around on the vessel took some ignoring.

Harbour-master Gor was intrigued to hear about the dark-clad Salamonite who had bested Captain Terrai on her own ship, and he resolved to prove to her that he was a more worthy opponent. As Darkmane made his unsteady way down the passenger gangplank, Gor appeared at the landward end.

'Stand still right there!' he said in his most officious voice. 'Where do you think you're going?' Darkmane stopped but said nothing, his eyes fixed firmly on the harbour-master. 'Lord Azzur, our beloved ruler, has a new rule about people like you. No one is allowed ashore during Whitewolf Fortnight. We don't want for-eigners here, not while we're celebrating the founder of our great city. You'll have to go back. Now.'

Darkmane held his ground. Sooner or later, he knew, the official would get around to explaining a way round the rule, a way that always involved exchanging coinage. He waited, a placid expression on his face. Behind him, he could hear the other passengers assembling at the head of the gangplank, ready to disembark. Their anxious whispers did not carry far enough for him to make out their words, but he had a good idea what they were saying.

Gor folded his arms. 'Well, what are you waiting for? Go on, go back. I'm sure Mistress Terrai will let you hire a bunk in the bilge for a reasonable sum,' the harbour-master sneered.

Darkmane realized that this time a bribe was not what was required. 'Begging your pardon, sir, but to where should I go back?' he asked humbly, trying not to let a smile break through his calm.

'Go back to where you originally came from, of course. What kind of an idiot are you?' The harbour-master rocked back on his heels and gazed around, plainly hoping to bask in the delight of an amused audience. That there wasn't one didn't seem to dampen his good humour.

'Where I came from?' Darkmane replied in a clear voice. 'But sire, I came from here.'

'Eh?'

'I said, I came from here.' Darkmane hunched his pack higher on his shoulder and stepped forward. 'So if you'll just let me pass, I'll be on my way. Good night to you, sir.' He stepped off the end of the gangplank and on to dry land again for the first time in three weeks.

'Oh no you don't! Not so fast,' the harbour-master blurted out a little too hastily, grasping Darkmane's sleeve. The latter stopped in his tracks and turned to stare at the sweaty hand as if it were something scraped off his boots. 'Where's your permit, stranger? No one gets past me without a permit signed in triplicate by Lord Azzur himself!'

Shadowmaster

With a twist of his upper arm and a flick of his other wrist, Darkmane turned the tables. Now, before he had time to draw breath, Eril Gor found himself held tight; one arm was slowly crushing the air out of his throat while the other reached down to pluck his dagger from its sheath and toss it out of harm's way.

Chadda Darkmane spun the harbour-master around again and grasped him by his upper arms. As he began to speak, his dark eyes blazed in sudden fury. Gor stepped back a pace as Darkmane raged, but the warrior kept on without pausing for breath. 'That's it; I've had enough! I've tried being civil, but now I've had more than I can stand of you and your snivelling tricks. I am Chadda Darkmane of the city of Salamonis and you've made me angry. I have been at sea on that perpetual wave engine for the last three weeks. I have been threatened with robbery and death and have avoided both only by the narrowest of margins. Before that, I risked death and madness to destroy a foe the likes of which you could not imagine in your wildest, most drunken nightmares. In going through these experiences, I have had my whole view of life changed irrevocably. And yet I have taken all these things philosophically. But *you*, you pathetic little worm, *you* have made me angry. And now you are going to pay.'

Eyes rolling to the very edge of his vision, seeking but not finding anything or anyone to aid his plight, the harbour-master took a step backwards, then another. Darkmane advanced, his teeth set in a grimace, his eyes as wild as lightning. Gor tried one last trick: 'You won't get away with this, you know. I only have to call out for help! Guaaaaaaa—'

Then Gor fell backwards over the edge of the quay. A few seconds later there was a splash as he hit the water.

Footsteps

Darkmane reshouldered his pack, turned and strode into Port Blacksand.

The number of people causing the footsteps had increased to four during the last minute. The new pair appeared to be some way ahead of the others and to one side; someone was creeping along in an alley behind the ramshackle buildings that loomed on either side of him. Darkmane kept walking. The encounter with the swindling harbour-master had destroyed any residue of goodwill left in his body; heaven help anyone who got in his way now.

He did not react when, from a smaller lane a little way ahead, a scrawny black cat ran, hell for leather, across his path, squealing in panic. A second later, a starvation-thin dog followed it, baying for its blood. So quick they could have been nothing but illusions, they and their cries were swallowed up in the silence.

The street led to a bridge across the river which divided Blacksand in two; it was lit with paper lanterns placed every few paces. Had he been in a better mood, Darkmane might well have amused himself by pondering how the footpads trailing him would cross the bridge without being seen by their quarry. Or he might have listened to the eerie sound of the breeze blowing through the skeletons that were impaled on the struts of the bridge as a grisly – but generally unheeded – warning to Port Blacksand's wrongdoers.

Darkmane did neither, marching on at a pace so rapid that those following him had to run to keep up. Halfway down the ramshackle street leading from the river, however, a surprising sight made him stop. The cat and dog which had crossed his path earlier now lay in an awkward heap in the mud a few paces in front of him.

Footsteps

Darkmane still looked directly ahead of him, but his hand went to the sword which hung at his side; normally when he was travelling it would have been strapped across his back, but Darkmane knew that Port Blacksand could confront a stranger with shocks and surprises.

'Hear this!' Darkmane's voice rang out between the high, overhanging buildings. 'I am Chadda Darkmane, of the city of Salamonis. My journey has been long but has some time yet before it is over. I will not be delayed here. Go now and you will live. Stay – and you will die.'

His words were answered by a low chuckle from high above him. Darkmane whirled, knife poised, handle up. His arm snapped forward and the blade flew like an arrow. A body dropped heavily into the dirt by the dead animals.

Suddenly they were upon him, darting like shadows from a breeze-blown candle. Darkmane tossed his pack aside and took a firm grip with both hands on the hilt of his longsword. He whirled around and took the first assailant in the side. A twist of the hips and another of the wrists, and his sword sliced through the wrist of the next. A hairy, taloned hand fell to the floor, still clutching tightly its serrated dagger.

Darkmane ducked his head, then snapped back upright, and the next footpad, running to stab him in the ribs, was tossed over his back and sent flying head over heels. There was the sound of something dry snapping. Whirling to face his next opponent, Darkmane found himself holding off two of them. Both were hooded and had dark cloths tied round their faces so that only their eyes were visible. One held a sword, the other an iron-bound club, but neither was as confident as he had been scant seconds before. The club-wielder committed himself to a lunge at Darkmane's head, plainly expecting his fellow to join in and attack at the same time. Finding himself fighting alone was almost as much of a shock as the sensation of cold steel sliding under his ribs.

The last footpad began to back away, legs sidling like a crab's. For as long as it took for his steady heart to beat once, Darkmane considering letting him go, but then his anger returned once more. As the robber turned to run, Darkmane leapt alongside him, growling, 'You had your chance!' The hooded figure turned and struck feebly at his opponent. Darkmane sidestepped the blow easily, and his own swing struck home.

Pack safely back on his shoulder, the knife returned to its hidden pouch up his sleeve and his sword sheathed by his side, Darkmane stalked away. He was muttering, to himself more than to anyone else, 'I'm sorry. I shouldn't have done that. You did have your chance, but I shouldn't have done that.'

Ahead of him lay the main gate, and beyond that the road began which would eventually take him home. Perhaps he would have to draw his sword once more before being allowed to leave this damnable city, perhaps not; but nothing was going to stand in his way, not now.

4

Finding Patterns

'STAY RIGHT WHERE YOU ARE, OLD MAN!'

The order, barked in a confident, high-pitched voice, came from a little way down the overgrown forest path. Though he peered ahead into the golden gloom of early evening, Yaztromo could not yet see who had given the order, but he had been expecting to meet someone on this path before he reached Oldcastle.

'Hail to you, whoever you are,' he answered. 'If you are kin to Norska Val then I come in peace.'

'I was indeed kin to our chieftain, Galana bless him,' the voice replied.

'Was?'

'Aye. He fell nobly two days since, defending our village from the attack by the accursed bandits and their foul leader. But if you are from around these parts you will know of this already.' There was the faintest of rustling sounds in the undergrowth, then a woman stepped on to the path. She was of average height and build, with dark hair cropped short in the manner of a boy. Her clothes were mottled green and tan, which explained how she was able to hide so well in the thick bushes, and she carried a small bow with an arrow notched, ready for firing.

'I am Yaztromo, and I make my home south of Darkwood. Although I knew of the attack, I had not heard of its sorry outcome, which is what I had come here to discover, among other things,' the old wizard replied.

'Yaztromo! You have not been seen in these parts for many a year; I cannot recall seeing you since I was a girl, but certainly I know of you. Oh yes, I have heard the tales they tell of you.' Yaztromo bowed his head modestly. 'I am Morin, daughter of Harn the trader. If you will follow me, I will lead you to our village.'

'Thank you, Morin. If you would be so kind as to wait a moment while I summon my pet . . .' Yaztromo put two fingers into his mouth and whistled three, long, high-pitched blasts.

'Your pet?' Morin winced as the whistling reverberated inside her head.

'Yes, but do not be alarmed; he is quite harml–'

'Yaaaz! Yaaaz!' A raggedy black shape hurtled down through the tops of the trees. With a yelp of alarm, Morin raised her bow to defend herself, but Yaztromo grabbed her wrist before she could fire. With much flapping of wings, the shape settled down on to the old wizard's shoulder.

'Morin, let me introduce Vermithrax, my pet. A pet who is going to get his tail-feathers shot off again if he is not careful!'

'Aw Yaaaz,' the bird replied. 'Three whistles means danger, so I came back to fright off nasty Goberlings. C-crawk!'

'No, you crazy avian! Two whistles is danger. Three just means come back to me. When will you learn?'

Finding Patterns

Yaztromo noticed out of the corner of his eye that Morin had started to giggle, and he sighed with exasperation. 'Come on. You lead the way, Morin. Let's go.'

The great hall of the old stone keep was crammed with bodies, laid out on all available floor-space. The injured were being tended by several grim-faced men and women who moved quietly from patient to patient and there was a hush in the air, as solemn as a temple.

Morin led the newcomer through the hall and into the gloomy room beyond. Here an exhausted-looking young man stood hunched over a table, poring through the latest in what was plainly a long series of scrolls by the light of a single sputtering candle. He was heavy-set, with a shock of blond hair through which a large hand repeatedly pushed strong fingers. His clothes, tattered and torn in many places and overlaid with random pieces of armour in a similarly ramshackle condition, looked as though they had been slept in for several days. The room itself matched his appearance; evidently it had been ransacked in a great hurry. Some attempt had been made to tidy up the furniture, but piles of broken wood and other fittings had simply been swept into heaps along the walls.

As Morin and Yaztromo entered, the man raised his weary head and gazed at them uncomprehendingly for a moment; then he half smiled a greeting to Morin. 'Hail to you, Morin. And who is this fellow?'

'Jemar Val, this is Yaztromo. He was a good friend of your father's in times past.'

The man brightened somewhat and peered at the old man. 'Why, so it is! Welcome, welcome, sorcerer. The last time I saw you I couldn't have been shoulder-high to a new-born horse.'

'So it is you, Jemar,' Yaztromo replied. 'You have the look of your late father about you, that is for certain. Are you to be the new chieftain of Oldcastle?'

'Aye, for the moment at least. When the village is back on its feet, if it ever is, I will ask its people to choose a new leader, but for now I am the obvious choice in the absence of anyone better.'

'Your father's old sparring partner, what was his name, Redhair? Surely he will advise you well?'

'Cormis died from his wounds yesterday morning,' the young man answered with a shiver. He glanced quickly up at Yaztromo. 'So many have died here, and for what? A mule's back worth of old silver and gold? It seems such a terrible, terrible waste! To think that the precious lives of all my family and friends were only worth their tiny share of so little.' He slumped back in his chair; at that moment it seemed as if he was carrying the entire weight of the tragedy on his own shoulders.

After a moment or two, Morin ventured to ask, 'Jem, how is your sister? Is she any better?'

If anything, Val's shoulders drooped even further as he shook his head slowly. 'There is still no change. She drifts in and out of her daze, but she rarely makes any sen—'

At that moment, from the very back of the chamber, a weak voice called out, 'Fa ... fath ...' At once, Jemar was on his feet, hurrying to his sister's side.

Now that his eyes were drawn to the gloom at the far end of the room, Yaztromo could see a narrow bed there. The figure lying upon it was very slight, more like a broken doll or puppet than a human, and one of her arms was bound up in a sling. She was deathly pale and gaunt of face, drifting on the shadowy borders between life and death.

Finding Patterns

Morin leaned over and whispered in Yaztromo's ear. 'Sullina, Jemar's sister. She was discovered after the battle, lying beneath the corpses of two of the accursed bandits. It was plain to all that she had killed them both, but she nearly paid for her heroism with her own life. Since she was discovered, she has remained in the sorry state you see her in now, oblivious to all our attempts to revive her.' Morin stole a peek to where Jemar mopped his sister's brow with a cloth, but it was plain that he did not hear her. 'Some have said that she has been transported to another place, where her ailing spirit is still in battle with the ghosts of those she killed, and only when she has won this second battle will her life be restored.'

Yaztromo strode over to the bunk. Passing his hand over the end of his staff, he commanded it in a soft voice to produce a gentle light. Now that he could see Sullina more clearly, his eyes took on a hard expression. It was plain to Morin that he did not like what he saw.

'You say that . . .' Yaztromo started to address Jemar but realized at once that the man would not respond; he turned to Morin and began again. 'You say that you have tried everything? Who has been treating her?'

'Our healer was killed in the marketplace, early in the raid, but her assistant has been doing whatever he can. Most of our wounded have been recovering according to plan. Wounds have begun to heal, broken bones have been set, everything as usual. With Sullina, though, none of the traditional methods have been working. Perhaps it is true what they say . . .'

Jemar spoke, his voice a low croak. 'I am sorry, Yaztromo, that my welcome has not been as courteous as it could have been, but I am at the end of my tether. I have been scouring father's scrolls, trying to find a clue as to how we could treat my sister, help her in her battle, if that really is what is needed. When I was a young boy, my father used to tell me that I must learn to read, for the scrolls held the answer to every question I would ever need to ask.' The man turned, his eyes brimming with desperate tears. 'But I've been through them, every single one, and I cannot find the answers to any of my questions! How could the scrolls lie? How could my father lie?' Jemar put his head down upon his comatose sister's bed and wept quietly, his shoulders shaking with each sob.

Yaztromo leaned forward on his staff and placed a comforting hand on his shoulder. 'Don't lose heart, Jemar Val. Your father was a great friend of mine in his younger days and, I have no doubt, you shall prove likewise. I have some knowledge of healing lore. If you will permit me, perhaps there is something I could do.'

The young chieftain recovered his composure a little. When he turned and gave his assent, a vague hope showed behind his eyes, though it had to fight for space with Val's overwhelming despair and fatigue. 'Do anything that will not harm her. My father spoke of you as he spoke of so few men. I know you will do your best.'

Yaztromo bowed his head. 'Thank you.' He turned back to Morin, who was eagerly shifting from foot to foot. 'Now then, these are the things I need: firstly, a handful each of the following herbs, manbane . . .'

'Manbane?'

'Don't interrupt!' Yaztromo snapped; Morin looked suitable abashed. 'Manbane, allium, entwarm and golden sails. You will remember all this, won't you?' Morin nodded eagerly, determined to do her very best. 'Very well. I will need a large leaf of yellow cabbage, two whole funnelwort, some fine thread and a needle. And plenty of boiling water. All right, off you go. Call on everyone who is free to help you; the sooner I receive all of these items, the sooner I can get to work.' Morin turned to go. 'One last ingredient – half a dozen lanterns or candles; it is going to be a long night.'

The sun had just slipped behind the trees as Chadda Darkmane descended the last hillock and stood once more outside Yaztromo's lofty tower. His cheery mood was dampened by the absence of any light showing, especially when this was combined with the derelict appearance of the upper levels of the tower. The fire, which had marked the start of his mad chase across the continent in pursuit of the thief who had stolen Yaztromo's scroll, had all but destroyed the top of the sorcerer's tower. The birds he kept for spying on the shadier denizens of Darkwood Forest and which dwelt in the large, glass-roofed aviary had been scattered over a wide area, and the wizard's miraculous far-seeing telescope had been so badly buckled that all he could see through it was a kaleidoscope of blurs.

Darkmane walked the last few paces up to the immense oak door. As always, it looked strong enough to repel an army if that was what its owner wished. The bell and gong were both present and correct. Keeping his eye on the small viewing panel set above them, Darkmane rang the bell, using the small hammer provided. He was becoming agitated. He had half expected that Yaztromo would have rushed out to greet him before he was half-way to the door. But even now, after the ringing of the bell had echoed away into the evening air, nothing at all happened.

So much for a glorious homecoming! Darkmane thought to himself, a wry smile creasing the corners of his mouth. *I had been hoping to stay here for a night or two,*

*telling Yaztromo all about the successful conclusion to my
mission. The Hamakei would have told him all about it
weeks ago, I'm sure, but Yaztromo would have sat patiently
while I went through it all again, and maybe again.*

*Ah well, if he really isn't here, I suppose I should push on
for Salamonis.* Darkmane looked at the darkening sky.
There were far too many stars to count. *In the morning,
in the morning . . .* He began to look around for a suitable
place to make camp.

Yaztromo turned and spoke to the man worriedly pacing
across the tiled floor of the chamber, keeping his voice
soft so as not to wake the woman who was lying asleep
on the narrow bunk next to him. 'You can stop looking
so anxious, Jemar Val. She is out of danger now. She has
won her fight, if you like.'

'That's —'

'Shhh, man. You'll wake her. What she needs now
more than anything is pure, honest sleep — and she
won't get that with you whooping your head off!'
Yaztromo hissed. 'Come on, help me to my feet and we
will return to the great hall.'

'Master wizard, I am in your debt.' The overjoyed
young chieftain looked as happy as a puppy, all trace of
weariness and worries gone, at least for the moment.
'What can I do to repay you? Just name it.'

Yaztromo patted his hand. 'All I need at this moment
is a cup of strong herbal tea and a soft rug to lie down
on. Your sister isn't the only one who needs her sleep.'

'Of course. I will see to your bedding personally. Ah,
here's Morin, and I think that steaming flagon should be
just what you need.'

Morin tiptoed across, careful not to spill the contents
of the mug. 'Here we are, Master Yaztromo. Begging

your pardon, sir, but by the look of you you could do with this. Your pet is in the kitchens telling two of the village guardsmen a tale about a one-armed swordsman and a singing horse the likes of which I never heard in my life before!'

Yaztromo chuckled. 'I warned you what you were taking on when you offered to entertain him! That bird grows more incorrigible every day. Where he gets it from I simply can't imagine.'

'Nor can I,' Morin giggled to herself. As she turned to go, she suddenly remembered something else. 'Oh, your pet mentioned that you might also care for this, sir.'

She thrust something soft and spongy into the sorcerer's hand, before skipping back in the direction of the kitchens.

Yaztromo peered down at his hand and was delighted to find she had brought him a large, sugar-coated cake. He smiled to himself. *The perfect reward! Perhaps I won't turn that bird into a pebble just yet.*

Late next morning, Yaztromo was summoned to a council of war. Jemar Val was there, looking as bright as a newly minted coin. Just as the dawn had broken, he informed the sorcerer gleefully, his sister had opened her beautiful green eyes and wished him good morning in a faint but defiantly alive voice! Also present at the council meeting were four of the village's remaining elders, including Cormis Redhair's widow, Aleen, and two Dwarfs. After they had all delivered their greetings and personal thanks to Yaztromo for his part in restoring Sullina to health, the meeting commenced.

Val began by summarizing what had happened during the bandit raid, from time to time calling upon one of the others to clarify some point about which he was unclear. Habul, a grizzled old Dwarf who was usually to be found making and selling all manner of fine jewellery and other metal items in the marketplace, described the closing moments of the raid in a gruff voice that was full of fiery passion. While Jemar Val was grieving for his dead father, the bandits had availed themselves of the contents of the keep's treasure room.

'They thought they had cleared all of us out of the way,' Habul said, 'but my young son, Biltur, managed to secrete himself behind one of the tapestries and eavesdrop upon them. What he has reported to me makes it plain that these bandits were not after our treasure at all. Or, rather, they were, but only a single item!' Habul paused for a moment to let the gravity of his claim sink in, then he continued. 'My son, young though he is, swears that he heard their ghastly leader command them seek out "the skull".'

'Skull? What skull is that?' Aleen Redhair asked in a surprised voice.

'I know not, lady, but it is plain from my son's report that after searching each and every corner of the room they eventually found what they were looking for. Biltur heard one of them shout to their leader, who gave a whoop of delight that sent tiny knives down the spine of my son, or so he told me. The leader cried, "That is it! That is it!" He told the finder that he would be well rewarded, then added, "One more, my fine fellows, just one more and our work is done."'

'What did he mean by this, do you suppose?' Jemar asked.

'I know not.' Habul shook his grizzled head. 'Soon after, the leader gave the order for his men to withdraw, taking all the treasure and their wounded with them. Before we knew it, they vanished, as rapidly as they had arrived, curse them!'

'Yaztromo, you know more of these matters than any of us, I would hazard,' Jemar said, turning to the wizard. 'Can you make any sense of all this?'

The old sorcerer had sat silently, leaning back in his chair and listening to each of them tell his or her part of the bandit attack, keeping his counsel until they had told all they had to tell. Now he rose to his feet and leaned forward over the table. All those round the table looked expectantly at him.

'I do not know what these bandits were after, but if the lad's spying is to be believed — and I see no reason not to believe him — it is plain to me that this was no ordinary bandit raid and these were no ordinary raiders. Their leader knew exactly what he was after even before they arrived here, and he used all his evil cunning to get it, while convincing all of you that this was just another raid. That is sure enough. What is also sure to me, as it must be to you, is that there will be another raid. Now, if we could work out where that will take place, we could make plans in advance to deal with it.'

'Begging your pardon, but what concern is that of ours?' the trader, Velm, interjected. He was a reed-thin man who had somehow come through all the fighting without sustaining a scratch. 'We sent riders to raise the alarm in the nearest villages — but, in their wisdom, our neighbours thought it best *not* to send a single man to our aid in our time of need. They know there are bandits abroad; what more need we do?'

Yaztromo fixed the man with grey eyes that held the lustre of freshly forged steel; the trader shrank back in his chair. 'When the news of the raid upon Kierdale reached you, what was your response, trader?'

'Well,' Velm stammered, playing for time, 'there was a meeting, and it was all decided quite fairly. We could not spare the men, nor . . .'

Finding Patterns

'Fairly?' Aleen Redhair spat out. 'You twisted the council round your little finger by promising a loss of trade and threatening to recall your crippling loans. Only Cormis and Norska were honest enough to stand against you, Churla Velm! We should have sent warriors to help. Mayhap we could have stopped this raid against our village before it ever happened!'

Sensing that young Jemar Val was unable to keep the meeting in order, Yaztromo raised a hand for calm. 'What is done is done. The situation, I would suggest, is very different now, and any vote that this council makes would have a very different result. But that is for you to decide at the appropriate time. For now, if there is going to be a raid, we must try to determine where it will be.'

Scraping back his chair, the trader stood up. 'I will have none of this. You will have to make your decisions without me!' He strode out, oblivious to the relieved smiles on the faces of those he left behind.

Yaztromo continued as though nothing had happened. 'Now, let us consider the raids that have occurred in the last few months. Until today I was unsure whether they were all connected, but now I think that that conclusion is the only one possible.' The wizard reached down into the bag lying at his feet and pulled out a rolled-up chart. Opening it, he spread it on the table and weighed down the curling corners with cups and a broken chair-leg; it proved to be his crudely drawn map of the area between Darkwood and the Moonstones. Leaning over the map, he pointed out a small mark labelled 'Oldcastle'.

'Master Yaztromo, forgive me,' Habul said in an unapologetic voice, 'for I cannot read anything save Dwarfish runes. Could you read out the names for me?'

'Of course I can. Here is Oldcastle, where we are meeting today.' Yaztromo's finger slid down and to the right across the parchment, until it rested upon another crudely inked spot. 'The first raid which I would unhesitatingly attribute to these bandits was upon Tegris, here, by the Silver.' The others craned their necks in order to see. 'There has been a peace of sorts in the region for several years. The warring Orc and Troll tribes had been lured south to fight in the Trolltooth Wars, and most of the rest of us have managed to exist without having to slaughter one another over the least little dispute. Suddenly, however, there were numerous reports of frequent raids on caravans and settlements in the Moonstones – and then these raids. The second was on Oakwall, which is about here.' He jabbed at the spot among the hills due north and some distance from Tegris. 'Then there was the recent raid upon your neighbours at Kierdale.' His finger tapped on another unmarked spot close to Oldcastle.

'Pardon me for interrupting, Master Yaztromo,' Jemar Val interjected, 'but your map is inaccurate.'

The old wizard peered across at him in silent surprise. It was an act of rare bravery to question his vast and all-encompassing knowledge. The Dwarf, Habul, turned to him and asked, 'What do you mean, lad? Speak up!'

'Well, sir, Kierdale is two days' hard ride from here, and so cannot be placed anywhere like as close as you have put it. Furthermore, it is to the north-east of us, I believe, not due north. Similarly, Oakwall is almost directly to the west of us, several days beyond the Lowland Gap.'

'By Kerillim's blessed silver hammer, he is right!' exclaimed the other Dwarf, Stoneharrow. 'Your chart is good enough, Master Wizard, but it is old and crude, and it does not show the true lie of the land.'

Yaztromo made a non-committal grumbling noise in his throat.

Finding Patterns

'Wait! Among my father's papers there is a newer chart, prepared only a few years ago. I will fetch it.' With that, Val jumped from his chair and hurried from the room. Yaztromo leaned on the table, peering at his faithful old map with an expression of slight embarrassment on his face. Within a few moments Val was back, a cylindrical scroll clutched in his arms. 'Here we are. Help me spread it out. Now,' he continued when it was spread on top of the wizard's chart, 'that's better. Begging your pardon, Yaztromo.'

The sorcerer waved away his polite apology and pored over the new map. 'Aha, well I never, you are quite correct, if this map is to be believed. Here is Tegris – I got that right at least. And Kierdale is here, almost due north of it. Here is Oldcastle, of course, and over there, due west of here, that must be . . . Oakwall . . .' Yaztromo's voice trailed off. They did not need to hear any more. They all saw it, there, where the imaginary lines their minds drew connecting the four raided villages crossed. Where the unknown cartographer had drawn a small but distinct silhouette of a stylized village, carefully sketched with crenellated walls over which poked a pair of buildings. Alongside it, in the same neat hand, he or she had inscribed the name of the village.

'Drystone.'

5

Drystone

'You are certain they will come?'

'Oh yes. There is no doubt in my mind that they will come here, and soon. They have had four days now to regroup, and if they are truly seeking the one last piece of their puzzle they will be eager to finish the job. They will come in force, and they will stop at nothing to gain what they came for.'

'And what is that last piece to be?'

'I know not, Chorn. An artefact of some sort from your treasure room – though I have searched through it a dozen times and have found nothing that I would swear could be the object they seek.'

'Well, Master Yaztromo, if they come, we will be ready for 'em. We have alerted those in the outlying farms who swear fealty to Drystone or to my family; I expect them to be here in number by sundown.'

Erl Chorn was the chieftain of the village, a stocky half-Dwarf whose family had dwelt in Drystone for many generations. He and Yaztromo were standing in the wooden lookout tower that had been constructed on the roof of his manor house to keep watch for raiders.

Drystone

Drystone was perched on the brow of a low hill in the very middle of a wide, wooded valley that was known locally as the Lowland Gap. From the top of the tower the two of them could see for many kilometres, though much of the view was hidden behind swathes of trees.

'Riders were dispatched on the road to Chalice last night as soon as the council voted to accept your account of the imminent attack as being true. If they manage to get fresh horses at Hallon and then ride through the night, they will be in Chalice by dawn tomorrow. They should be able to raise enough reinforcements to enable us to hold off a fair-sized army, let alone a mere bandit rabble.'

Yaztromo leaned forward a little, shading his eyes against the sharp sunlight which had just broken through the clouds to warm the morning. 'They will not be in time. Look.'

Erl Chorn followed the sorcerer's pointing finger into the near distance, to where the first large copse of trees hid the path eastwards. Figures were moving quickly along the path, making for Drystone. He swore under his breath as he counted the bandits. 'So soon? And we are not yet ready!' Hands forming a hood over his eyes, he scanned round the edge of the trees in the other directions. 'More of them are coming from the west; they must have circled round us last night. Curse it! We sent scouts in all directions, to forewarn us of this. Why have they not reported?'

Yaztromo gathered his flowing robes round him and began to lower himself cautiously down the wooden ladder which led to the lookout tower. 'Because they were no match for the raiders. You are not dealing with a fair-weather brigand who will try to make off with your horses and geese in the middle of the night. Ring that bell and sound the alarm. Hurry, hurry.'

Shadowmaster

Chorn's hand was already on the rope. The discordant clanging of the alarm bell began to echo across the village.

His feet had grown accustomed to the numbness that hours of walking along bumpy tracks had induced, but Darkmane was mindful to rest awhile as soon as he felt the first pangs of real fatigue begin to creep up his legs. Swinging his pack and sword from his back, he sat down on a small grassy hillock not far from the path, pulled off a muddy boot and began to rub some life back into his aching foot. The grass was still a little damp from the rain that had fallen during the night, and Darkmane had been glad to get shelter in the small farming village yesterday evening. This thought in turn reminded him of the bundle of food stashed at the top of his pack.

As he chewed on a hunk of bread topped with a slice of powerful-tasting goat's cheese, Darkmane tried to draw a picture in his mind of where he was. The kindly miller who had allowed him to sleep next to the fire last night back in Hallon had pointed out the path which would eventually lead him to Chalice, and thence to distant Salamonis. The miller had been full of awe at the thought of anyone venturing as far as the city. He and his wife thought he was taking his very life in his hands every time he made his twice-yearly trip to Chalice, and they and their children had a great many questions to ask about the far city. Was it true that the roads were paved with cobblestones fashioned from pure gold, and that King Salamon wore a crown covered in so many diamonds and other jewels that he could barely hold his head up? Although tired and grimy from the road, Darkmane answered their questions as truthfully as he could, though when the family settled down to sleep he was still uncertain whether they had believed a single one of his denials.

Back in the direction from which he had come, Darkmane's ears picked up the unmistakable sound of horses' hoofs coming along the path. Hastily, he wrapped up the remnants of his food and pulled his boots back on. It did not pay to be trusting on these roads; there was no guarantee the riders would be friendly, or even human. As the sound came nearer, he ran a little way down the path to where a clump of trees offered a place for him to hide. *Four horses, at a canter*, Darkmane's senses told him. *They must have come through Hallon, so they may well be friendly. Perhaps I can beg a lift*, he smiled to himself.

The riders came into view. There were four horses, as Darkmane had deduced, but only two bore riders. Both were human, a man and a woman, dressed for travelling but with the sun-browned, ruddy complexions of people who were used to working the land for a living. When they were still some way distant, Chadda Darkmane stepped out from among the trees and raised one hand in greeting. The other gripped his sword half-way down the scabbard; it would take but an instant to have it in his hand, were it needed.

'Hail!' Darkmane called as the riders drew up. 'A fine day for travelling. Do we share the road to Chalice?'

'Hail to you, sir.' The woman spoke with more than a trace of wariness in her voice. 'If you are headed for Chalice, you do indeed share our path this day.'

'I am Chadda Darkmane of Salamonis, and I have been walking for days. Could I ride with you?'

The man spoke up, his voice deferential but cold. 'Master Darkmane, you are nothing if not to the point! Some might almost consider you ill-mannered. You will forgive us, then, if we are equally abrupt. We are riding for Chalice on a matter of the utmost urgency, in search of reinforcements to defend our village from an expected attack. Every moment we delay could cost Drystone dear. We have not just bargained ourselves these fresh horses in Hallon in order to give them away to the first stranger we meet on the road.'

'Drystone, you say? Who do you suppose to be attacking you?' Darkmane asked. 'If that is not an impolite question.'

The man bristled and plainly was about to say something even more impolite in return, but the woman laid a hand upon his arm and replied for him. 'Forgive our haste, but it could be a matter of life and death. The wizard Yaztromo has . . . what?'

In a split second Darkmane was fully alert, every fibre of his being attentive. He grabbed the reins of the nearest horse. 'Yaztromo? What of him? Tell me! Tell me now!' Seeing their surprise, he added quickly, 'He and I are friends. I am returning at present from a mission he himself dispatched me upon. I had hoped to rejoin him at his tower in Darkwood several days ago, but when I arrived there he was not to be found.'

The man leaned forward, fixing Darkmane's eyes with his own. 'Prove you are friend to the wizard.'

Darkmane's mind raced. 'What would you have me do? I can tell you that he has long white hair and beard and the oldest eyes of anyone I have ever met. He is tall of frame and stout of build; too stout, if the truth be told, from feasting upon sugared cakes whenever he has the opportunity. If I know Gereth, he will be accompanied by a bird, Vermithrax by name, a pet crow who is his life's bane – yet one of his greatest loves too. What else would you have me tell you? Ask away; if Yaztromo is involved I would offer help at once, though my life depended upon it.'

Drystone

The two leaned together, whispering. It did not take them long to reach a decision. The woman spoke for them: 'We are convinced. I did not know his first name was Gereth, but everything else you say is true. He arrived at our village of Drystone yesterday, and managed to convince the elders that we were all in imminent danger of attack by bandits who have been responsible for several other attacks in recent times. We have been sent to raise reinforcements among the adventurers and mercenaries of Chalice, and hopefully to return in time.'

The man added, 'Will you accompany us to Chalice? An adventurer like yourself will be of the greatest help in tracking down others like you to assist our village.'

Darkmane, however, had already made up his mind. 'No. My place is alongside Yaztromo, if trouble is brewing. Give me one of your horses and tell me which paths I must take, and I will ride for Drystone immediately.'

'How goes it?' Yaztromo panted to Chorn.

'Badly, very badly!' The half-Dwarf was spattered with gore, though he did not appear to have sustained any injuries himself. 'We must retreat into the manor house immediately if we are to have any chance of holding out against them.'

'But you will be depriving yourself of an escape route if you do that. You will be like too many fish in a tub, and they will stand over you choosing their targets in the certain knowledge of spearing you,' Yaztromo countered.

'I am not so sure, wizard. These are not ordinary bandits, as you have told me many times in the last twenty-four hours. Now I have solid proof of this. They are toying with us!'

Yaztromo turned to gaze at him. 'How mean you?'

'Unless their commander is a complete fool, I would have to say that they are fighting for sport, for practice. Each time we fall back, they fail to press home their advantage. Instead, they turn on their heels and slowly but surely pick off all those trapped among them. What is more, they are taking prisoners!'

'You are sure of that? No, of course you are. Yet I have not heard that they took any prisoners in any of their previous raids. Just what is going on?'

Chorn shook his head, rubbing crimson-streaked sweat from his brow. 'I know not. If they are merely after our treasure − and the object they seek − they are taking their time about it. Because they caught us before we were properly ready, we have taken very heavy losses. We are a disorganized, inexperienced rabble compared to them, yet it is only now that the fighting has concentrated on the centre of the village and the manor house.'

Yaztromo peered out into the gloom of the village. There was still a goodly portion of the afternoon left, but thick clouds from the fires of a dozen burning buildings obscured most of the sky. Occasionally blurred figures ran or rode in and out of the smoke, fighting or fleeing.

Yaztromo and the Dwarf, along with a small number of Chorn's kin, were inside a large barn close to the manor house. The air was thick with the smoke of burning wood and straw; and within Yaztromo's mind another cloud was obscuring the scene. He had been trying for hours to reach out with his magic; using all the power he had stored in his staff before embarking on his journey, he should have been able to read the scene of the battle as clearly as if it were under the glare of the brightest beacon. Moreover he ought to have gained some knowledge of the enemy's intentions and plans before they were carried into action. But a fog like a dense blanket lay across the scene, making every probe of his mind feel as though he was wading waist-deep through treacle. Another power was at work, that was plain, but his swamp-slowed mind could not get to grips with it. Now he was growing exhausted without even the scent of success.

Chorn continued his report; though he was the village chieftain, it was plain that he deferred to Yaztromo as ultimate leader of their defences. 'Since they are supposed to be seeking this artefact, I was contemplating surrendering and allowing them access. Now, though, it is plain to me that we must fight on. If they are taking prisoners, for whatever reason, we cannot surrender.'

The sorcerer grasped Chorn's shoulder in a surprisingly powerful grip. 'That is right, Erl Chorn. You cannot surrender, though the situation will get far worse before it gets better.' Yaztromo relaxed his clasp a little. 'Come. Let us repair to the manor house and call in those you have called your commanders for their reports on the situation. Mayhap they will provide us with some much-needed inspiration.'

'Lord, it is as you said. They pulling back into big house. Those that live.' The immense Troll smiled wickedly, but the gaunt-faced commander did not appear to have heard him. He stood, one hand absently worrying at one of the long, talon-like fingernails on the other, the thin smile fixed on his face as always.

'Lord . . .' the Troll ventured.

'I have ears.' The voice was calm and rounded; but it had the peculiar quality of sounding as if the words it spoke were travelling across vast distances of time, so that whatever the voice said demanded and was given the utmost attention.

The lumbering Troll bowed awkwardly and stepped back a pace, then snapped to attention and remained silent. He knew what happened to insubordinate troops. As a Troll, he could appreciate the finesse with which his sinister master wielded abject terror. The master would consult him when he was needed, he chided himself; how dare he presume otherwise? The Troll tried, with little success, to stop his massive body shivering at the sudden panic which gripped him.

'There is a sorcerer with them.' The leader spoke aloud, accustomed to being listened to without question. 'I have felt his tiny mind bumbling around like a puppy let outside for the first time. Fool. Little does he know that Axion is already beginning to rejoin himself, that the power within the Bloodstone is already strong enough to throw a cloud across this place. When the final piece is in our hands, we will be unstoppable.'

'Yes, lord,' the Troll ventured.

'How many prisoners do we have?' the commander asked, turning his full gaze on his second-in-command for the first time. 'Have we enough?'

'More than enough, living and dead. As you instructed.'

'Very well. It is time to fetch what we came for. Give the order to attack the manor house.'

The sight that greeted Chadda Darkmane from the top of the valley filled him with despair. The gloom of evening was lightened by a myriad fires, and the greying clouds were hidden by spiralling columns of thick black smoke. *No! I cannot be too late! Surely I am not too late!*

Drystone

Gereth! Darkmane patted the neck of his exhausted horse and urged him on.

'Come on, boy. One last effort. It is all downhill from here. Do not fail me now!'

He slapped his legs against the horse's flanks and the tired beast tried to protest. Darkmane was a master horseman, however, and knew how to tug on the reins to make his mount do exactly what was required of it. Horse and rider picked up speed until they were galloping full pelt down the sloping path that led to Drystone.

Close behind him, unobserved in the dusky light, a host of dark riders gave chase.

With one powerful slice of his great axe, the Troll leader severed the head of the first villager inside the double doorway of the treasure room. As it collapsed to the floor, the headless body clawed at the air as if fighting to stay upright. Before it struck the floor, the Troll had kicked it aside and was swinging at the wide-eyed warrior who stood behind it. His motley band of raiders surged into the room behind him, howling insanely and brandishing their crudely forged weapons wildly.

There was a retina-searing flash round the doorway, and a wave of unnatural-coloured flames swept towards the advancing enemy. Three bandits fell back, faces disfigured beyond recognition, the fire leaping hungrily across bubbling flesh. More raiders pushed past the dead and dying. Yaztromo retreated behind a pillar in order to recover his strength. He felt so tired, as though every little effort was draining his life away. In a sudden moment of calm he wondered where Vermithrax was. All round him the battle continued its bloody progress.

In one corner, a husband and wife defended a window against three Orc-things which were trying to gain entry to the hall. The villagers' swords, crudely fashioned by the local blacksmith but sharp enough to pierce leathery hides and inhuman skulls, swung and lunged again and again. A green, taloned hand was severed and fell into the room, still clutching its spiked club, and rank blood splashed in all directions. As the howling creature fell back, a chattering Lizard Man pushed up, jabbing its spear through the opening. The defenders ducked round it and struck again and again with their swords.

The fiercest battle was by the door, where the Troll commander and his most loyal followers were slowly but surely carving their blood-soaked way into the hall. Chorn and his hand-picked escort of burly Dwarfs were fighting a losing battle amid the chaos. A half-brother went down, gore pouring from his neck. Another duelled with a scimitar-wielding Goblin, their blades flashing back and forth between them until the press of numbers in the room separated them, sending them towards different opponents. Chorn himself fought heroically with his trusty two-headed axe, accounting for more than half a dozen of the enemy before falling back behind the main crush of battle to rest awhile and recover his strength.

Here he was joined by Yaztromo. The old wizard looked drawn and trembling but still allowed the half-Dwarf chieftain to lean on him and recover his second wind. Behind them, hanging on the wall, an ancient, dust-heavy tapestry showed a battle-scene very like that being played out before them.

'I fear we will lose everything,' Chorn panted. 'They are overwhelming us. We will fight to the last, but I fear we are lost.'

Yaztromo nodded his head. 'I wish it were not so, Erl Chorn, yet it seems the situation is hopeless. We will all die here.'

Drystone

Chorn roused himself, his strength returning to him. 'Aye, wizard; but if I am to die, let me die defending Drystone. I will take another dozen with me before I am gone.'

Before he could dart back into the fray and carry out his vow, Yaztromo's hand clasped his shoulder, and the old man hissed in his ear. 'Wait! What is this? Something comes!'

The front ranks of the enemy continued to press into the room, but behind them the crush had moved to create a space. Through the gap, striding confidently among the recumbent bodies of the dead and the dying, came the bandit leader. He was in Shapechanger form, dark leathery skin glinting almost regally in the blood-soaked half-light within the hall. He moved as though he had not yet noticed the savage fighting scant metres ahead of him; or he had noticed it but did not care to acknowledge it. Towering over his troops and their opponents, he peered round the hall, oblivious to the clash of steel and the screams of agony that continued to clamour all round him. His jet eyes scanned back and forth, seeing far more than mortal eyes ever could.

Yaztromo's mind was suddenly assailed by a white-hot spear of magical energy. He was pinned against the wall by the full force of the assault, and it was all he could do to stop the beam from pushing right through his mind. With the force came a soft chuckling, a voice reeking with such malevolent arrogance that the wizard felt his sanity begin to fray at the edges. Gathering all his willpower, Yaztromo managed to twist his mind out of the path of the magic. Nearly destroyed by the effort, his ageing body slumped against the wall and he slid to the ground. Chorn barely had time to cry out in alarm before being assailed by an immense Orc swinging a razor-tipped flail at his exposed head.

Behind the insensible wizard, cracks began to appear in the plaster wall and the ancient tapestry rippled and flapped like a flag in a gale. Pieces of stone were shaken loose as the wall, buckling under some unseen pressure, shuddered and creaked. Accompanied by a horrible, shrieking, scraping noise, the wall burst asunder, showering bricks and dust all around. Many fell to the ground, temporarily stunned. What happened next stilled the shouts of those who were still conscious. The tapestry, shredded as if by dragon claws, parted like a pair of curtains and a small, metal-bound chest flew out across the room, above the heads of all present.

The Shapechanger bandit leader snatched it out of the air with a grunt. His talons skittered on the metal binding then held it firm. 'I have you! I have you!' he howled in delight.

'And you will pay for it,' a stern voice rang out from the doorway behind him. Chadda Darkmane strode into the room, sword raised, its tip already making a trajectory that would lead it eventually to a point somewhere at the back of the Shapechanger's throat. Behind the mercenary came a motley rabble of farmers and other locals, all determined not to arrive too late.

Pushing a stray flake of brick from his shoulder, Yaztromo spoke aloud: 'Darkmane!' But his voice was lost among the cacophony as the clamour of battle recommenced with a crash in the room like a wave against a cliff-face.

Darkmane swung again and again, his trusty weapon humming through the rank air, trying with all his might to land a blow on the darting figure of the Shapechanger. The latter slashed out with one cruelly clawed hand, the other clutching the precious chest to his body. The monster grabbed a nearby creature and flung it at

Shadowmaster

Darkmane: it was a small Goblin, and the human barely had time to dodge it. The Shapechanger leader's talons slashed at his opponent, gouging three parallel grooves in his chainmail but, luckily, not managing to penetrate his skin.

Darkmane stepped back to steady himself and brought his sword down at the monster's exposed head. To his surprise, the creature caught his sword in the valley between thumb and forefinger. Darkmane's muscles bunched and he dragged down with all his might, while the Shapechanger tried to keep the sword from cutting down, through his hand and on towards his spiny head. Their eyes locked, both totally oblivious to the battle which continued to rage round them.

Darkmane's arms were made of steel, it seemed, and they would not buckle. A thin growl escaped his lips. Slowly, almost imperceptibly, the edge of his sword began to slice down into the Shapechanger's hand. The creature's triple-forked tongue flickered in his gaping mouth as he struggled to resist Darkmane's strength, knowing now that he was losing. Heaving new breath into his lungs, Chadda Darkmane pushed his screaming muscles to new heights of effort. His sword slid deeper through the creature's tendons; he could feel its progress trembling up through the weapon and into his arms. Within a heartbeat his sword would divide the creature's hand in two and slice down into its inhuman skull. Victory was his.

Then the world exploded in a warm flare of agony, and Darkmane slid to the floor.

The Troll second-in-command lowered his club and bowed to his master.

'Give the order to retreat,' his leader hissed through clenched teeth.

6

Well Met!

Consciousness returned to Darkmane ever so slowly. The chamber was silent, disturbingly so after the hubbub of battle. The floor was cold and hard under his back. He could feel blood trickling from the throbbing wound on his head.

He tried to sit upright. Silver stars flickered before his eyes and needles of bright agony lanced his skull. The movement brought a surge of nausea and he felt his stomach churn; the bitter taste of bile filled his mouth. He wanted to scream, to give voice to his anguish, as if by shouting out loud he could release the pain from his head. He steeled himself; such was not the way of a soldier of Salamonis. A true warrior endured in silence and thereby increased his Amonour. Darkmane gritted his teeth and willed himself to move. The effort was too much. He slumped back to the floor. Gnarled hands caught him as he fell.

'Careful, my young friend,' came Yaztromo's familiar voice. His care-lined old face swam into Darkmane's field of vision. Piercing, but surprisingly youthful eyes provided a stable point of reference. 'Don't over-exert yourself. You're lucky to be alive. Not many folk would survive having a Troll use their head for ogreball practice. It is indeed fortunate that your skull is so thick. Lie still; I have sent for the herbs I shall require to tend your wound.'

'Let go of me, enchanter. I'll stand on my own two feet without anyone's help. I need no sorcerous aid.' The pain made Darkmane short-tempered — that, and the knowledge that he had been struck down treacherously from behind. He glared around at the place where he had fought the monster. Everywhere, signs of battle were evident to his impaired vision. A pair of Goblin corpses lay, broken and twisted, near the body of a grizzled old farmer. A notched scimitar had somehow become embedded in a wooden pillar. A party of red-eyed survivors, their clothes begrimed from the battle, were dragging bodies from the room. The raw stench of blood and carnage hung in the air.

'Don't be foolish Chadda,' said Yaztromo. 'You —'

'I said, let me go, wizard. When I cannot stand up by myself, that will be the time for me to die.'

Even in his weakened state, he knew he was too strong for Yaztromo to restrain him. The old magician let go of Darkmane's shoulders. The swordsman slumped backwards and hit the ground hard. Agony blazed through his battered head.

'Perhaps this once I'll accept your help,' he muttered before darkness swept over him once more.

Yaztromo sat silently in a cracked wooden chair, salvaged from the burnt-out shell of the village inn. He looked down at the unconscious form of Chadda Darkmane, which lay near his feet on a mattress of straw covered in a grey field-blanket. At least he was going to be all right, he pondered; my healing skills still function. A simple poultice of spear-root and greyhelm had been enough to treat the wound. That was the one patch of brightness in this otherwise gloomy picture.

Yaztromo was surprised at the affection he felt for the infuriatingly self-confident young warrior. There was something about Darkmane that commanded respect, though: a poise, a self-possession that made you believe he was nearly as capable as he thought he was. Yet there was something more: Darkmane carried about him a sense of destiny, as if he had been chosen by the gods to perform great deeds. Mystery cloaked him. He claimed to hate magic, yet some of his closest allies and friends were mages, and he had shown considerable aptitude for wielding it in his conflict with the demon, Rivel. And there was his past; Chadda Darkmane never talked about his past, never mentioned friends or family − what secrets did he hold back?

Secrets, mysteries? I'm getting too old for such things, Yaztromo thought. His mood was black. The encounter with the evil creature who led the bandit force had left him with a premonition of doom. By all the gods, but the thing had been strong. The way his magical strength had been sapped from him was frightening. Yaztromo knew he was no longer a young man. As his body had grown older and weaker, he had come to rely more and more on the power of his craft. Now he had met a foe who could neutralize even that.

He felt helpless. He knew nothing of the foe with whom he had struggled and against whom he had lost. It was baffling. There were too many questions he could not answer. Why was there such a strange pattern to the bandit force's attacks? What exactly was it that the leader sought, and had it found what it was looking for?

Yaztromo smacked his fist into his palm in frustration. Knowledge, even more than spell power, was vital for a wizard. He hoped Vermithrax would soon return from his scouting mission. He needed to know the answers to so many questions before he could formulate a solution to this problem.

Darkmane felt better the next time he awoke. The back of his head was cold and numb, but the pain felt distant. He probed the area with his fingertips. A bandage had been wrapped round his head; it felt moist and sticky. He brought his hand round to the front of his face, expecting to see blood. A pale-white paste was visible on his fingers. It smelled vaguely of mint; medicinal herbs, he guessed.

'Where am I?' he asked in a croaking voice, glancing around. His surroundings were not familiar. He lay on the floor of a wrecked house. The stone walls were scorched and the thatched roof had burned away. A layer of fine ash had defied all efforts to sweep the room clean. Yaztromo slumped wearily in a heavy wooden chair. Near by stood two other seats, obviously salvaged from the ruins in the aftermath of the battle. 'What happened to the monster?'

Yaztromo sat in silence for long moments, his eyes fixed on some distant point beyond Darkmane's head. The warrior was used to the mage's distracted moods, but this time something was different: he sat stiffly and his eyes were sunken. Deep lines of weariness had etched themselves into his face. He no longer resembled the sprightly codger with whom Darkmane had spent many long hours in joyful philosophical argument. He looked like a man on whom the weight of decades, perhaps of centuries, had suddenly fallen. As Darkmane watched, he shook his head and emerged from his dark reverie. The movement was slight, as if he had been drained of all energy. He smiled, but his expression was weary and edged with pain and fatigue.

'You are in the home of Chorn the Half-Dwarfen, high chieftain and wardmaster of Drystone – or at least what's left of it. I fear my efforts at protecting my neighbours have been sorely lacking.'

Was there an edge of bitterness in the old man's voice, an admission of self-doubt that Darkmane had never heard before?

'At least we are alive and so, I suppose, must some of the villagers. I must have hurt the creature enough to drive it away,' Darkmane hazarded.

Once again the wizard shook his head. This time the motion was more emphatic. 'Hurt it? Yes, I suppose you did. Drove it away? No. My guess is that it got what it had come for. It achieved what it had set out to do and had nothing to gain by remaining. We were lucky, Chadda, lucky. After you fell, the thing could have destroyed us if it wished. It could have ordered the entire village to be slain, and I could have done nothing. Instead, it just turned and left. It led its troops away as swiftly as they had come. I have never felt so impotent. It was as if it considered me too unimportant for it to concern itself with.'

Darkmane had never seen his friend so disturbed. He rose unsteadily to his feet in spite of the weakness that spiralled through him. 'It is just another creature of the darkness. We have vanquished them before and we will defeat this one now.'

Yaztromo gazed straight into Darkmane's eyes. His voice was bleak. 'I know not, my friend. If this creature is an agent of darkness, then night may fall over this

land. I have felt the strength of its magic and it is mighty indeed. You do not know enough of my arts to comprehend the extent of its power.'

Darkmane's thoughts drifted back to his encounter with the demon, Rivel. He had fought the creature through the shadowy realms between the worlds and had triumphed over it by using magic for the first time. He remembered how, at one stage of the battle, he had felt helpless, and he shuddered at the thought of what would have happened if he had given up. He knew he had to shake the old man out of his black mood.

'You are wrong, Gereth. I have tasted its power now, and I no longer fear it. What I fear is the abuse of its power. If this monster is so mighty then we must oppose it. For if we cannot, who can?'

'Yes, my friend, who can?'

*

Chorn strode wearily through the doorway and glared suspiciously at the two companions. He advanced towards Darkmane and offered him his hand.

'I know not who you are, youth, but I must thank you on behalf of my people.' His voice held no warmth and his manner was frosty. It was clear that in some way he associated Darkmane and Yaztromo with the problems of his village, and their presence made him uncomfortable.

Darkmane rose and shook hands. The half-Dwarf had a bone-crushing grip. 'I am Chadda Darkmane, captain in the service of the King of Salamonis. Whatever aid I rendered was given willingly, for it contributes to my Amonour.'

Chorn's look became increasingly dubious. He gave the warrior a look that said, you are a vainglorious fool. 'Oh to be young enough to face death for the thrill of it,' he said humourlessly. 'Unfortunately, I have a family and other responsibilities.'

Darkmane bit back a retort. It was clear that the chieftain was tired and bitter with grief. Today he had fought such creatures as might blast a man's sanity asunder. The young warrior was more used to such encounters, while Chorn obviously was not. If he could not be courteous to a stranger, it was up to Darkmane to be doubly courteous.

'Your people fought bravely today,' he said.

'As folk will, to defend hearth and home. But at what terrible cost! Over half my kinsfolk slaughtered and a score more wounded. I blame myself: I should have surrendered when I had the chance. Much suffering might have been avoided.' The look he shot Yaztromo made it clear that it was not himself he blamed but the wizard.

'And then again perhaps not,' countered the wizard sharply. 'There is no sense in wasting our time on what might have been and could have been. We must concentrate on combating the evil at hand.'

'Perhaps you must, Yaztromo Spellsinger, but the folk of Drystone are done with combat. I'll thank you to –'

Outside, a warning bell began to sound.

As the sound of the alarm bell faded, Jemar Val gazed at the breached walls of Drystone and did not know whether to be disappointed or not. The acrid smell of smoke, mingled with the stench of burning bodies, assaulted his nostrils and made his eyes sting. It was obvious that they had come too late to take part in the battle. The part of him that thirsted for revenge on his father's killer seethed with frustration. The part of him that dreaded an encounter with the supernaturally powerful murderer was relieved. The knowledge that he had found among his father's scrolls inclined him to be more relieved than angry.

'Too late,' Aleen Redhair said softly. It sounded like a curse. Since the battle of Oldcastle there had been a hard set to her mouth and new lines surrounded her eyes. 'Wait — what's that?'

Jemar followed the line of her pointing finger, as did the eyes of every warrior in the hastily assembled relief column. His hand dropped to the hilt of his weapon. From out of the smoke a figure emerged: it was a surprised-looking human, garbed in a grimy, smoke-stained tunic and clutching a pitchfork with desperate courage.

''Tis a man, unless my eyes deceive me,' said Gillibran, the leader of the Stoneharrow Dwarfs, running his hand through his thick white beard. Like the folk of Oldcastle, he had brought every warrior who could be spared to help defend Drystone. Jemar was glad that the doughty Dwarf warriors were present. Gillibran gestured with his weighty war-hammer and ten Dwarfs advanced, their mail-armour clinking. 'And if any harm has befallen my old friend, Yaztromo, I will take it out on his hide.'

'Wait, I recognize him,' interjected Jemar. 'It is Lothar Buntz, the freeholder. Often did he reside as a guest with my father. Hail, old fellow, what news of Yaztromo, the enchanter of Darkwood?'

'He is within, Jemar Val, he and his soldier friend are with our chief in his home. Both are unharmed, praise Avana. They saved us from the darkspawn leader when all was thought lost.'

'The monster is slain, then?' Jemar asked hopefully.

'No. Seeing it could not overcome Darkmane, it snatched up its prize and fled like a common thief. The hero was struck down by a treacherous blow from its henchman and could not set off in pursuit.'

'This Darkmane must be a hero indeed,' said Aleen. Jemar's heart sank. The creature had escaped with its prize. Knowing what he now knew, he would say that made the prospects for the future look very dark indeed.

'Take me to the wizard,' he said. 'I have urgent news for him.'

Darkmane sat quietly and attempted to digest the news that Jemar Val had brought. The soft-spoken young man's words rang in his head. Their horror had not been lessened by the calm manner of their delivery. In fact, Jemar Val's certainty and the quiet resignation with which Yaztromo had listened to his speech made disbelief impossible. It only emphasized the fearfulness of their predicament.

'I have read of this Axion,' said Yaztromo, 'and none of the stories were good.'

Darkmane thought this an understatement, judging by what Jemar Val had said. Axion was a creature of darkest nightmare. An immortal, deathless sorcerer whose experiments during his twisted pursuit of eternal life had cost the lives of thousands. A monster so terrible that a dozen heroes had died attempting to kill him.

'According to your tale, the five parts of his body were each buried under the villages which have been attacked, Drystone and Oldcastle and the others?' Chorn's expression wavered between disbelief and out-right terror. Darkmane could tell that he desperately wanted to be able to ignore Jemar Val's story but that his experience during the battle made it impossible to deny the possibility of supernatural involvement. 'If he was unkillable, how, then, was he defeated? And if he was killed three centuries ago, what use could his bones be now?'

A reasonable question, Darkmane thought, and made more pertinent by the fact that someone had relentlessly sought possession of Axion's earthly remains. They must have some great supernatural significance. That much seemed clear to a man with even Darkmane's limited knowledge of sorcery.

'There are ways,' said Yaztromo. 'Spells that would neutralize his power long enough to allow warriors to overcome him. I believe the Hidden Mage must have cast just such a spell when she and Goran the Southlander stole into Axion's Keep.'

'And chopped him up,' added Jemar Val excitedly. 'Don't you see, all these centuries he wasn't really dead. The parts of his body were alive and buried in different places.'

'And now . . .' said Gillibran, who had remained stolidly silent all this time. 'And now someone has all the pieces, and –'

'And wants to put them back together again,' finished Yaztromo. Then, as if to himself, he added, 'But if the disciple is so powerful, what must the master be like?'

In the silence that followed, the hurried beating of wings could clearly be heard.

'K-raark! Well, Yaaaz, you were right. Headed east along the Grey Paths into Moonstones.'

The bird gazed around smugly. Its small eyes glittered brightly. It was the only being present in Chorn's ruined hall that did not seem infected by the all-pervading atmosphere of gloom.

Gillibran looked up. 'The Moonstone Hills? Along the Grey Paths, you say?'

'That's right, stumpy. That's what I said. You deaf? C-rrawk?'

The Dwarf chieftain's beard bristled. Like all his folk, he was proud and touchy. He raised his legendary magical war-hammer threateningly for a moment, then realized how ridiculous he must look, menacing a crow. 'The Grey Paths must eventually lead to Haellsgarth — the Hellsgate, in human tongue. 'Twas an ancient fortress of my people from a time when they were more numerous and had fewer dealings with men. They built the fortress inside a mountain peak; the lower levels are connected to the Brightloam Caverns. There's enough room inside there to hide an army.'

'And it's well hidden enough to perform magical rituals in secret,' added Yaztromo.

'Whatever nefarious activity this demon's disciple is up to, we must go and stop him,' said Darkmane. He smiled crookedly. 'We must halt this evil sorcery before it goes any further.'

One look at the faces of the others present convinced him that no one was keen to accompany him. Eventually Yaztromo spoke.

'You are right, Darkmane. We must do so.'

'It is suicide,' said Gillibran. 'The Grey Paths are a maze in which a man can wander for weeks. The Moonstones are haunted by Trolls and worse. Still, I can think of worse adventure. Count me in.'

'No, Gillibran', said Yaztromo. 'The duties of a leader are to his own followers. You must return to your people to prepare for the evil days which are coming. Young Jemar can advise you. The folk of Darkwood must be prepared. We might fail.'

Well Met!

'We will not,' said Darkmane. The tone of the wizard's voice had not reassured him. For a moment he had thought Yaztromo was about to say 'when we fail'.

7

Awakening

As he lifted the Bloodstone high above his head, Cawlis grinned balefully. His followers stood before him, their eyes downcast, unable to look directly on the visage of their terrible master. Within the circular jewel a dim light flickered palely, its cold glimmer illuminating the ritual components on the table.

To an eye less well versed in sorcery than Cawlis's, they would have looked like discarded, useless trash hoarded in the lair of a particularly stupid Goblin. They did not look like items for which scores of people had been killed and entire villages laid waste. On the rune-engraved slab lay the outline of a man composed of bones and dirt and bits of offal. The stench of decomposition filled the air. A shallow hollow had been left where the heart should be. Plump, off-white maggots wriggled through pieces of putrefying meat where the stomach should have been. Worms crawled through the sightless sockets of the horned skull. Cawlis smiled; the skull had been the last relic of the Great Magus he had recovered. It seemed so long ago now, though in fact it had been only a few brief days. But what was mere time to one such as the Great Magus? Whoever knew his secrets would be master of life and death, holder of the keys to eternity. Now he had all the relics: the skull, the eyes, the talons, the hand – and the Bloodstone.

'Ashaaak! Pentaak! Kalif! Null!' He shouted the words and they echoed eerily round the cavern. 'Hear us, oh Axion, and come at our call.'

At a sign from Cawlis, a red-robed Goblin leaned forward and applied essence of mirkweed to the figure outlined on the table. The creature's hands shook and a few drops splashed on the slab. They evaporated almost instantly, leaving a bitter, acrid odour in the air.

'Ashaaak! Pentaak! Kalif! Null! We call you, Great Magus! Come forth from your secret home!' A burly Orc acolyte poured the contents of two brass flasks on to the body and maggots were soon floating in puddles of perfumed oil. As they drowned and died, the jewel in Cawlis's hand glowed slightly brighter. Having finished his task, the Orc kissed each container and stepped back. The air became cooler and Cawlis could feel the first faint currents of magic begin to eddy in the charged air.

'Ashaaak! Pentaak! Kalif! Null! We call you, Eternal Spirit Lord! We beg of you: enter your prepared vessel.'

A Lizard Man reached into a cracked bowl, took the two handfuls of dust that were all that remained of an ancient king of Men and cast them into the air. The dust glittered in the candlelight, sparkling like fireflies. The candles dimmed as if the light were being sucked from them. The temperature continued to drop. The motes of dust swirled and then were sucked towards the gem in the Shapechanger's hand. The ripples of sorcerous energy increased. The gem blazed with the absorbed light. Shadows danced away to the far corners of the chamber. Cawlis's monstrous outline flickered mesmerically. A

faint scent of burning ozone was added to the warring odours filling the chamber.

'Ashaaak! Pentaak! Kalif! Null! We command you, live again, Dread Master of Mysteries. We bid thee inhabit this your host. By blood we bind you to your prepared vessel.'

Now all the followers present drew their daggers and made a cut into their right thumbs. Once the incisions had been made, they held their hands over the body and let droplets of blood fall on to the host. Where each red spot fell, it curdled with a sizzling sound like water dropped on to a red-hot skillet. As the curdled blood was absorbed into the shape on the table, it was moulded into a translucent red film which covered the whole mockery of a human form. Once the film had enveloped the entire creature, Cawlis reached forward and placed the Bloodstone over the hole where the heart should have been. Still blazing with light, it sank through the film until it was lodged at its heart.

As one, the occupants of the chamber froze in place.

Cawlis moved his arms through the vast sweep of the Ritual of Incarnation. He was filled with power now. He breathed it in from the magical heavy air. When he spoke, it charged his voice, distorting it and making his words resonate with eerie authority. This was the critical point of the ceremony. If things went wrong now, the result would be disaster. He had opened a pathway between two worlds. The outcome of such matters was always uncertain, and here he was trafficking with one who had mastered the forces of Life and Death. Yet he knew no fear.

'Hear me, oh Axion. By thy Skull I summon thee. Let thoughts once more fill thy head.' He pointed to the horned fragment of cranium, and an arc of purest magical energy leapt from his fingertip. The skull glowed incandescent for a second, then the magelight faded as it was absorbed by the relic.

A faint whisper filled the air. It was almost inaudible, but the sound of it made the Chaos creatures shudder. 'Who . . . iss . . . calling . . . ussss?'

'Hear me, oh Axion! By thine eyes I summon thee. May you gaze once more upon this mortal world.'

Energy flickered between Cawlis and the emerald gems that filled the Magus's eye-sockets. They blazed momentarily.

Another voice, different from the first, spoke up. 'Who Is Calling Us?' It was a voice to bring fear to the stoutest of hearts. It hinted at knowledge of the most unspeakable secrets. It was the voice of a graveyard creature newly returned from the dead.

'Hear me, oh Axion! By thy hand do I summon thee. I grant thee strength to grasp what is thine and to hold it against thy foes.' Cawlis started as the magic was drawn almost involuntarily from him, sparks of purple energy leaping to Axion's left hand.

'Who is calling us?' pleaded another voice, one that inspired pity by the tortured depths of its twisted suffering. Tears rolled, unbidden, down an Orc acolyte's cheeks.

'Hear me, oh Axion! By thy talons I summon thee and grant thee sharp weapons to smite thy foes!'

'WHO IS CALLING US?' roared a fourth voice, howling with such dreadful rage that the weeping Orc fainted dead away and the others cringed back in terror. Only Cawlis stood firm, undaunted by what he heard, luxuriating in the sublime current of magic being channelled through his body.

Awakening

'By thy heart I summon thee, oh Axion. Let it grant thee power and bind thee once more to this transient realm.'

The magic generated by the ritual hurtled into the Bloodstone with such force that Cawlis struggled to retain consciousness. The heart pulsed once, then continued to glow with a steady light. Within the blood-red film covering the body, faint tendrils of muscle sprouted within the putrescent meat. They flowed over the skeleton of filth like fast-growing ivy covering the branches of some particularly nauseating tree.

'Who is calling us?' asked a fifth voice, calm and measured and possessed of great wisdom. All the other voices echoed its words, again and again, growing ever louder as they twisted round and round each other. The entire chamber reverberated with their echoes.

'Who is calling us?'

'Calling?'

'Us?'

'Who? Who? Who? Who?'

'Iiiis!'

Each time the sentence was repeated, different voices spoke different words, sometimes even changing over in mid-word. The voices mingled and warred with each other. 'Who is calling us?'

'I am Cawlis. I summoned you, master. I brought you back. I gave you a body, that you may walk the world once more.'

The hand of Axion twitched. The maggots had extended into white veins and were boring their way through the thin layer of muscle. Axion's skeletal face grimaced as if in discomfort.

'Why did you presume to do this?'

'You made me, as you made all my kind.' Cawlis answered at once.

The jewelled eyes swivelled slowly in their sockets to focus on Cawlis. 'I perceive you are a Shapechanger. I created them in the early days of my experiments . . . in the first century of my life. Perhaps I did indeed make you. It has been so long and I have forgotten so much.'

'Not all your dark knowledge, I hope.' There was an ingratiating note in the Shapechanger's voice.

Strange, mad laughter rang out, laced as much with mockery as with self-hate. 'No, not everything. Not enough. Too much!' Suddenly the creature that was Axion lurched slowly and painfully to its feet. 'I am Axion, the Master of Shadows, Lord of the Hellsgate. Bow to me! All of you, bow!'

The terrified Orcs bowed low. The Goblin prostrated itself in terror. The Lizard Man made the tail-high gesture of obedience common to its kind. Cawlis, too, garbed once more in his slender human shape, bowed low and elegantly. The gesture hid a secret smile.

8

Finding a Guide

Stumbling once more, Yaztromo cursed the steep, rock-strewn path. If he had had any doubts over the wisdom of their journey, the route they had taken confirmed them. The way was simply a grey track, overgrown with moss and strewn with dull flinty pebbles. It wound serpent-like up the face of some of the steepest, bleakest and coldest hills it had ever been the sorcerer's misfortune to cross. The only sound, besides that of their boots scraping on the rock, was the whine of the thin wind passing through a nearby tree. Yaztromo stopped to inspect it; it was precisely what he would have expected to find here: near-leafless, clinging to the rocky hillside by its gnarled roots. It reminded him of nothing more than a bent and bitter old man frozen in place while trying to scale the mountainside. Maybe it was – such things happened in the wild areas of Titan.

Vermithrax's beady eyes glared down from one of the barren branches.

'K-raark! Tired already, Yazz? You're puffing like a blacksmith's bellows. C-rawk! Take more exercise! Eat less sugar cakes!'

'Thank you for your advice, you bird-brained ferret. I think it has come a little late.' The sorcerer was wheezing and his heart hammered against his ribs like a prisoner beating on the door of his cell. He steadied himself by leaning a hand on the tree trunk. The bark felt scaly beneath his fingertips. This high up, the cold nipped continually at his bare hands and nose. Waiting for his heart rate to slow, he surveyed the land visible round him.

Below, the hills sloped down to the edge of Darkwood, far away in the distance, visible as a great green carpet that rolled westwards as far as the eye could see. Nestling in the folds at the foot of the hills were many little valleys. Some contained pools fed by the streams running down the slope; indeed, they had stopped at one earlier to drink and replenish their water flasks before attempting this rugged trail. Yaztromo could still remember the tang of the ice-cold water on his tongue. It was one of his more pleasant memories of this morning, certainly better than hacking his way through the brambles while their thorns tore at his robe.

At this height they seemed very close to the clouds. A sky the colour of smoke blocked the sun and cast a shroud of gloom over the land below. Yaztromo prayed for a break in the cloud cover. The sight of even a single ray of sunshine would cheer him up in this frigid place. For the moment, however, his prayer went unanswered, as they so often did. Just for a second he wished he was sitting once more in the comfortable book-lined study of his tower. He did not like adventures; they were fine if you were young and fit like Chadda Darkmane, but singularly unpleasant if you were an old and overweight wizard used to his home comforts. It was most unfair of adventure to seek him out at his age. Why had it not knocked on the door of some lithe and limber young mage? Somehow it didn't seem fair.

'Stop dawdling, Yaztromo, we still have to find this Weasel fellow!' Darkmane's shout shook him out of his reverie. 'It was you who insisted we find a guide!' he reminded the wizard. Darkmane was now a considerable way up the slope, about to vanish over the brow of the next ridge. He presented a tall, black-garbed silhouette against the grey of the hillside. Yaztromo cursed his youthful energy. 'His cave's just over the way, the old lady said,' Darkmane added.

Yaztromo set his shoulders and trudged wearily up the hill. Vermithrax took to the air with a great fluttering of his midnight wings and cruised off in Darkmane's direction. Yaztromo briefly considered flying himself, but he decided it would take up too much of his magical energy. He hoped this Weasel was as good a guide as the old woman had claimed, back at her farm. He'd better be, after all the effort they'd put into finding him!

As the noose was slipped round his neck, Weasel decided that the situation had got somewhat out of hand.

'Er, lads, I don't like this game any more. Do you think we can stop now? I think you've made your point. A joke's a joke, and this one's been very funny, of course . . . ha ha . . . but you've taken it just a little too far.'

'What makes you think we're joking, Weez?' enquired One Eyed Hef, a sour smile making his thin face look even less handsome than usual. Weasel didn't like the tone of mocking politeness in his voice, but now didn't seem to be the time to point this out. Already his calves were starting to ache from balancing precariously on top of the tall pointed rock.

'Yeah?' shouted Big Jax. 'What makes you think we're jokin', eh?'

Weasel could see his point. The hulking bravo wasn't exactly famous for his sense of humour. To be more precise, he wasn't exactly famous for sense of any sort. He certainly couldn't be expected to see the funny side of the way Weasel had so cleverly sold them the local chieftain's horse back in Angrim.

'Look lads, I'll pay you back, honest. You know I'm good for it. I've got a secret stash of gold right near here. Just let me down and I'll nip off and get it.'

'That's what you said in Wintermere − then you led us right into that Ogre's cave and scarpered. I've still got the bruises.' Privately Weasel thought it very churlish of Gotrud to bring this up. But then he expected nothing better from the overgrown Goblin.

'I'm glad you mentioned that. I've been waiting for a chance to clear up that misunderstanding. You see ... Urk!'

His words were cut off by Hef jerking the rope tight. He was forced to stand on tiptoe just to be able to breathe.

'I bet you have, Weez. I bet you have. While you're explaining, why don't you tell us why you told Eric Whitehand and his boys that we were bounty hunters come to look for him down in Gnollwood. It took me weeks to get over the kicking they gave us.'

'It was an honest mistake,' whined Weasel. 'Can I help it if Eric's got a bad temper and his lads are a little over-protective? Um, what's this?'

He looked down at the sickle Hef had placed in his hand. It was old and rusty and none too sharp. Sweat ran down his back; he wasn't sure whether it was from fear or the strain of balancing on his toes for so long. Probably both, he decided.

Finding a Guide

'You were right, Weez. We are going to play a little game. I'm sure you'll enjoy it.'

'Yeah, you'd better – or we'll bash you till you do.'

Suddenly Weasel understood. The big rock. The noose slung from the nearest tree. The sickle. Yes, they were going to play a game, one with Weasel's life at stake. Damn it all! He wished they hadn't caught him asleep in his cave. He wondered how they had found him. Maybe he shouldn't have boasted of his exploits to that old woman. Maybe he shouldn't have nicked that bottle of grog from her. Maybe he shouldn't have drunk himself senseless last night and lain asleep all morning with a hangover.

Oh, it was all so unfair. What had he ever done to deserve this? It didn't seem right that the world should be deprived of anyone as brave and handsome and clever as himself. Why did the gods always victimize him so?

'Now, Weez. I'm just gonna kick this rock away and then you'll be danglin' nicely at the end of the rope – where you should have been years ago, by the way – then it gets real simple. All you've got to do is cut yourself down 'fore you strangle.'

'A ploy worthy of one of your great cleverness, Hef,' Weasel whispered through his constricted throat. 'But may I suggest a slight variation. Just to make it sporting. You don't kick the rock away. That still leaves me with the incredibly difficult task of sawing through the rope with this blunt sickle you have provided. It's possible I might die of old age before I manage it.'

'You can't talk your way out of this one, Weez.'

'As if I would even try, Hef. How could I possibly fool a man of your insight and perception? It's the thing I've always admired most about you, by the way. That and your great charm.'

Hef shook his head. 'No use, Weez. You'd better save your breath. You're gonna need it.'

Weasel glanced around at their coldly set faces. They meant to do it: they intended to stand by and watch while he choked to death on the end of the rope. By the gods, they were cruel. And after all the things he had done for them, the ingrates. 'One last question?'

'Fire away, Weez. It ain't gonna save you.'

'What happens if I do cut myself down?'

The three bandits fingered their weapons evilly. 'Then we kill you anyway.'

'That hardly seems fair.'

''Bye, Weez.'

'Yeah! 'Bye, you little rat.'

'May a thousand Dwarfs bite your earlobes in the nether regions of the pit,' added Gotrud.

Hef kicked the rock. Ever so slowly it tipped over. The rope pulled burningly tight round Weasel's throat. His feet kicked futilely in empty air. He knew he was about to die.

Chadda Darkmane hurled his knife. It flew true, tumbling end over end, towards the rope. The razor-sharp blade sliced cleanly through the twined hemp. The little man the bandits had called Weasel dropped unceremoniously, to land on the rocky earth. He gave a great squeal of fear. 'No, I'm dead. I'm dead!' he howled. 'I'm too young and handsome to die!'

The three bandits looked on, open-mouthed. They stood, frozen with amazement, as Darkmane stepped out from behind the tree and leapt lithely down the rocky slope to confront Weasel's attackers. He landed nimbly on the balls of his feet, absorbing the impact with a slight flexing of his knees. His sword was in his hand. It felt as heavy as death and as reassuring as a friend's voice.

'Begone,' he said softly, 'and I will spare your lives.'

Weasel gaped up at him. His mouth twisted, as if he were trying to say something, but the words failed to come out.

'Who do you think you are, mate?' asked the one called Hef. 'You've just bought yourself a world of trouble.'

'I am Chadda Darkmane. Soldier of Salamonis. Vanquisher of Zharradan Maar. Banisher of the demon prince, Rivel. I can assure you that if you oppose me you will surely suffer.'

'Why, if it isn't my old pal, Yoda Darkmoan,' Weasel choked. 'Now you're in trouble, Hef. He's the greatest swordsman in all of Salmonella. Go on, Yoda, sort them out.'

Darkmane looked down at the pock-faced little man in astonishment. He had never seen him before in his entire life. This Weasel was certainly quick to capitalize on an opportunity, he had to admit. Even as he spoke, he was crawling backwards, away from the potential fight.

'You, worm, stay where you are!' roared Darkmane. The sheer force of his command stopped Weasel in his tracks.

'My name's Weasel,' he sniffed affronted. 'You should know that, Darkmoan. Old buddy. Old pal.'

'In case you ain't noticed, there's three of us and only one of you,' said Hef. 'Hardly sporting odds, wouldn't you say?'

'You're right,' Darkmane agreed. 'You had best send for five more vermin like yourselves.'

Weasel gave a great false laugh at what he perceived to be Darkmane's joke. Then he realized that the tall man wasn't joking. The others came to the same conclusion. They shuffled their feet uneasily, daunted by Darkmane's sheer self-confidence.

'Besides, gentlemen, he's not alone,' a new voice butted in. It was deep and hoarse and redolent of ancient wisdom. 'I am with him.'

Weasel had to admit the old coot knew how to make an entrance. He stood on the rocky outcrop from which this Darkmoan had just leapt, his cloak flapping in the wind, a great wooden staff clutched in one hand. Perched on his shoulder, a huge black crow spread its wings. A nimbus of light played round the tip of the staff.

'It's old Yaztromo, the wizard of Darkwood,' muttered Gotrud. 'He once drove away my entire tribe with fireballs. I don't want to fight him.'

'Nostromo, mate! Long time, no see!' croaked Weasel.

Yaztromo pointed his staff at the bandits. Hef and his boys turned and fled.

'It's not that I'm ungrateful, you understand. I mean, you did save my life and all that – but, let's face it, a man's got to eat!'

'A purse of gold,' muttered Yaztromo. 'It's outrageous. I could hire two Elf rangers and a troupe of dancing girls for that.'

'If you can find them, I'd be grateful,' said Weasel. He raised an eyebrow in what he obviously believed to be a gesture of some sophistication. The effect was only slightly spoiled by the way he licked his thin lips with his slimy pink tongue. 'Specially the dancing girls, you know what I mean?'

Darkmane shook his head in disbelief. The man had no concept of honour, let alone Amonour; he sought only money. He reached for his sword menacingly.

Weasel looked at him unworriedly. He had guessed, quite correctly, that Darkmane was not the sort of man who would kill him out of hand.

'Why do they call you Weasel?' Darkmane asked.

'Because I'm sleek, cunning, tenacious and brave, of course.'

'I'm glad you told me that. I was starting to think it was because you were sneaky, odious and thoroughly vile.'

'There's no need to get abusive; it's you who wants a favour, after all. Like the old girl told you, I'm the best guide this side of the Moonstones. In fact, I'm legendary round about here. Just ask anyone. I know these hills like the back of my hand. And you have to pay for quality, you know what I mean?'

Now that the danger was past, the slender little man strutted around as self-importantly as a bantam cock. Darkmane wondered privately whether he could possibly live up to his own assessment of his worth. Well, the old woman had certainly seemed impressed. The tales she had told about Weasel couldn't all be lies, could they?

Yaztromo shrugged his head in a gesture of resignation and reached for his purse. 'Very well. We'll pay.'

Darkmane caught his friend's wrist in a steely clasp. 'We'll pay *after* you have led us successfully to our goal.'

For a moment Weasel looked abashed. 'No can do, old mate.'

'We'll just have to go alone then.' Darkmane ignored Yaztromo's astonished look.

'Suit yourself. I don't give credit. No exceptions. Never. There are too many tricksters about. No credit — it's my one inflexible rule.'

'I always do suit myself, Weasel.' Darkmane said nonchalantly. 'By the way, if you should see your friend Hef again, do pass on my regards.'

Finding a Guide

'What do you mean?' asked Weasel nervously.

'Well, he and his delightful associates are bound to be still lurking round here somewhere.'

Weasel considered for a moment. 'On the other hand, you know, rules were made to be broken.' He smiled winningly. 'After all, you did save my life.'

9

A Nice Quiet Job

'This wind could cut through flesh,' Harrek said bitterly. He pulled his cloak tighter round him against the breeze. It was no use: the chill seeped right through the heavy wool and numbed him to the bone. His fingers were so cold he could barely hold his horse's reins. He gestured back to where the wagons straggled along behind him. 'Five silver pieces a day isn't nearly enough for this sort of work. I think I'll ask old Fatguts for a raise.'

'You knew the rate of pay when you signed on to guard this caravan. Can't change your contract now,' Sabrin replied calmly. Her eyes were slits as she scanned the surrounding terrain. Tears ran down her sunburnt cheeks, the cold wind making her eyes water uncontrollably. Sabrin had said exactly what Harrek had expected her to say. She was an old hand at this game, had been a mercenary for twenty years. She had served with such legendary characters as Konrad Halfhand and Pelgrim of Salamonis. To her, a job was a job. She endured it stolidly and waited to collect her pay. Whether the trip was a pleasant ride through the sun-dappled summer paths round Darkwood or, like this one, a frozen march along the edge of the southern Moonstones, she managed to keep up the same stolidly indifferent front.

Looking up at the forbidding rock-faces to the north of them, Harrek decided that what she lacked most was imagination. This countryside would give an Ogre nightmares. It was the bleakest place he had ever seen in his two-year career as a mercenary. There was very little life here, only tenacious lichen that covered the slate-coloured rocks, and the occasional stunted tree that somehow managed to put down roots in the patches of thin earth. Every so often, great jumbles of rocks covered the ground, rounded boulders that seemed to have been piled on top of one another by giant hands.

No imagination: that was definitely Sabrin's problem – but the same could not be said of him. He had grown up with his mind inflamed by the tales of adventure told by the storytellers in the West Market in Salamonis. The peaceful city had been too dull for a boy raised on a diet of legends that spoke of mighty deeds and hidden treasures. He had desired to emulate the heroes of old rather than slave away all his life among the lasts of his father's cobbler's shop. He could still remember the night he had stolen away, carrying a rusty broadsword that had belonged to his uncle and wearing the cloak his mother had patched a thousand times. At the time, thrilling adventures had seemed just round the corner.

He had travelled through Darkwood with the first caravan of traders he had been able to sign on with, venturing as far east as Kulak. He had done his share of fighting and adventuring, but he had yet to find the stuff of legends, to perform the heroic deeds of which he had dreamed. He had earned enough wealth to buy a new red cloak, a decent sword and a miniature painting of his sweetheart, Yanna, a tavern keeper's daughter in

Oldcastle. He smiled when he thought of the girl. She wanted to marry and to settle down, but he knew he could not just yet. He had still to find what he sought, the stuff of heroic adventure. It was what he wanted more than anything. Maybe this time. He looked at the rocks lying all around.

'Looks like a good spot for an ambush,' he said. 'Best keep our eyes peeled.'

Sabrin shook her head. 'You worry too much. Too cold for bandits on a day like this. Don't worry about it: you'll be in front of the fire, quaffing ale with your girl tomorrow night, no problem.'

The Troll commander heard the sound of approaching hoofbeats and smiled. It was almost too easy. His master, Cawlis, had been correct: the humans had followed the route exactly as he had predicted. His scouts had been stalking them for hours, checking that they would pass this point of ambush. A rich merchant and his guards, by the look of things: rich pickings. That would please his lads.

He counted the numbers. No more than a score. More than enough to discourage a band of hit-and-run raiders, but not nearly enough to stop the force that lay in wait for them among the rocks. He hoped none of the Orcs would jump up too soon. It would be just like one of those animals to go and give the game away. He swore an oath to himself that if one did – that idiot, Blashak, for example – he would personally tear his ears off.

The humans were close enough now for the Troll to make out a young man's voice. 'I'm telling you Sabrin. I'm going to ask him for a raise. We take all the risks, he makes all the money.'

'What risks?' answered a woman's voice. 'This trip's been a stroll in the park so far.'

A Nice Quiet Job

'Ready?' the Troll commanded. 'Let's go. Now!'

Harrek almost froze in his seat as the first Orc leapt down upon him. His attention had wandered off into a daydream about killing Dragons when the jabbering creature suddenly appeared beside him as if from nowhere. Where had it come from? The rocks, he thought quickly, pulling his sword from its scabbard just in time to parry the sweep of the creature's crude axe. Steel rang on steel, sparks flashing as the blades met. From all around came the sound of battle: war-cries, Orcish howling and the screams of the merchants as they tried to control the wagons.

Harrek aimed a cut at the Orc and it ducked. Out of the corner of his eye, he saw Sabrin struggling to control her startled horse. Harrek guided his mount with his knees and it reared to bring its weight down upon his attacker. Harrek ventured a look around. A ramshackle horde of Orcs, Goblins and other unsavoury creatures had emerged from among the rocks. They were hideous things, their scaly faces surrounded by ruffles of tendrils or marked with warts and mottled like toads. In their taloned claws they brandished a motley assortment of old but serviceable weapons. There were many dozens of them, a green-skinned tide washing across the grey rock.

Individual details burned themselves into his memory. A Lizard Man's tail lashing as it stood, poised, on top of a boulder. The bandaged arm of a nearby Goblin, the grey wrapping marked with a crust of dried green blood. The odour of unwashed bodies mingling with the leathery smell of the Orcs themselves. The sensation of bone crunching under his horse's hoofs. Everything seemed to be happening in slow motion, as in a nightmare.

He heard Sabrin yelling near by, her voice cracking
more in surprise than fear. 'There's too many of them!
What are they doing here? This was supposed to be an
easy trip!'

There was a puzzled note in her voice, as if life had
played a trick on her that she couldn't understand. She
sounded disappointed, as if an old friend had let her
down. She still wore a puzzled frown as the Lizard Men
dragged her from the saddle.

Harrek rode to her aid, but it was too late. The
monsters had already begun to feast. All he could do
was bring his blade down on the nearest creature. Its
head sailed away into the rocks and a liquid fountain
sprayed into the air. He turned his horse in order to scan
the battlefield and knew then that his position was
hopeless. There were far too many of the raiders for the
small force to cope with. It made no sense: there were

too many of them to gain a profit from attacking so small a caravan. Harrek shook his head. He knew at that moment that he was going to die. He would never see Yanna again, never go on a mighty quest. That being the case, he resolved, he would make one last stand fit for a hero. With a great cry he charged into the fray. There were tears in his eyes, tears that were not caused by the cold wind.

The Troll gazed down at the red-cloaked body of the yellow-haired young human. By the Dark Ones, he had been a worthy foe. He had butchered a dozen Orcs before being knocked from his saddle. Even after his legs had been hamstrung, he had managed to down two Lizard Men. Finally the Troll himself had had to move in and had taken several deep cuts before the battered warrior had fallen. He had indeed been a mighty foe.

Shadowmaster

The Troll opened the locket he had taken from the dead man's neck. He hoped it would contain something to make the scars he had gained worthwhile, a treasure of some sort, maybe something magical. All it held was the picture of a human female. The Troll decided to wear it anyway. It would remind him of his victory this day. He watched his followers wrap the bodies carefully in the winding sheets.

'Careful now,' he ordered. 'They must be fresh and unmarked. Or I'll have your ears!'

10

Star

'We've been wandering around in circles for four days now. Do you know the way or not, you snake-tongued piece of Troll offal?'

Darkmane grasped Weasel by the lapel and hoisted him into the air with one hand. The little man dangled there, feet kicking backwards and forwards futilely. Darkmane could not remember ever being so angry. There was something about Weasel that just set his teeth on edge. It could be the endless stock of very repetitive lewd tales, or perhaps it was the constant barrage of boasting. Maybe it was the way his new-found companion always managed to wriggle out of doing his fair share of chores whenever they set up camp. Or perhaps he simply didn't like the noxious little toady.

The trip had started well enough. They had followed the path from Weasel's cave along a slow, winding route that rose by degrees into the hills. The terrain had become less bleak as they made their way into an area of sparse forest. During the first day Weasel had even managed to knock over some rabbits with an improvised sling.

Shadowmaster

Darkmane had begun to have his suspicions about the man's qualifications on the second day when Weasel picked some toadstools for breakfast. He had claimed that he had eaten them dozens of times and that they were delicious for breakfast. Yaztromo had gently pointed out that they were speckled deathcaps, one of the most virulently poisonous fungi known. One bite was enough to kill a man. Weasel made a great show of inspecting them before announcing that the wizard was right after all. That day they had grown so hungry that Weasel had suggested eating Vermithrax. He had ceased his efforts to convince them that a nice crow stew would make a good meal only when the mage's familiar had threatened to peck his eyes out.

Later that day he had confidently announced that the tracks of a deer had been made by wolves and he had advised to turn back. Both men had spent enough time in woods to recognize the tracks of wolves. By the third day, it had become obvious that Weasel was simply picking paths at random. He would confidently announce that they would soon come to this stream or that circle of standing stones, but they never materialized. He had told them tales of how mighty pine trees grew from little acorns and how bears like to lurk in trees before dropping down to surprise their prey. He had said all of this with such confident ease that most folk would have been tempted to believe him. Darkmane was convinced that their so-called guide knew as much about forests as a herring would.

'Going around in circles?' Weasel spluttered. As usual when he was frightened, he glanced around frantically, as if searching for a way out or hoping that help would suddenly appear. 'You insult me, sir! How can you say that?'

Darkmane gestured towards the glade with his right hand. Even when angry he always kept his weapon hand free. 'Because this is where we made camp this morning. Those are the remains of our campfire from last night.'

'I'll grant you that to the untrained eye there's a certain similarity, but that is not our campfire. Trust me; I'm a professional. There must be other travellers passing along this way.'

'Other travellers? Going towards the Hellsgate? Looking to get themselves killed by our sorcerer friend?'

'Yes — I mean, no! Maybe they are his allies. Yes, that must be it — they are his allies. Often when sitting round the campfires we have heard tales of such folk. If we hurry, we may be able to overtake them. If you put me down, that is.' Weasel glanced imploringly at Yaztromo, seeking to enlist the wizard's help in freeing himself.

The white-haired old man stroked his beard thoughtfully. 'Is it not odd that three sets of bootprints leave here? One set is my size. One is Darkmane's size and one is the same as yours.' Yaztromo pondered. He raised his head to the skies and cocked it to one side as if listening. He had dispatched Vermithrax to scout out the land as soon as they entered the glade and saw the ashes of the burned-out fire.

'Now that is a coincidence,' said Weasel. 'It's a funny old world and no mistake. What do you think the odds are against that: three travellers passing along our route with exactly the same size of feet? In all my long years as a professional guide in these hills I've never heard of such a thing. Let me down, Darkmane, old mate. I must take a look at these tracks ... make sure old Yaztromo hasn't made a mistake. His eyes can't be that good at his age, you know what I mean?'

Darkmane growled. It was a low, animal sound that came from deep in his throat.

Weasel went white with fear. 'That sounds like a nasty sore throat you've got there, Yoda, old mate. I know how you feel, believe me. I'm not a well man myself. It's all this sleeping on damp ground in the cold hill air. I've caught a nasty chill. Is it any wonder I might have made the tiniest of mistakes. But come on, I've got you this far, haven't I? I got you here.'

When Darkmane spoke, his voice came out slow and grating; every word had a ponderous emphasis placed upon it, as if the warrior was finding it difficult to speak coherently and had to concentrate all his faculties on pronouncing each word clearly. 'My name is Chadda. Chadda. But you don't need to remember it because I am going to kill you. Here and now. Where you stand.'

'Now, now, Chadda. There's no need for violence. I understand you're not well, what with your sore throat and all. You're coming down with a flux, that's what it is. If you look in my pocket, you'll find just the thing for it — a nice speckled mushroom. No? Well, just put me down and we can go our separate ways. No hard feelings. I'll only take half my normal fee.'

'Prepare to die!'

At that moment Vermithrax swooped down into the glade in a flurry of dark wings. 'C-rawk! Yaaaz! Yaaaz! Come quickly! Nasty monster! Killing people!'

The crow circled once, then flew back in the direction he had come from, but slowly enough for the men to follow. Darkmane dropped Weasel and whipped his sword from its scabbard. He and the wizard raced out of the glade. Behind them Weasel began to shout. 'See, I told you those weren't our tracks. I told you. Hey, wait for me! Don't leave me here on my own!'

The sounds of fighting ahead had stopped, and so had

the screams. Darkmane skidded to a halt as he entered the glade, his feet slipping on the soft loam. His heart was pounding slightly, more from excitement than the exertion. His anger with Weasel was all but forgotten, now that real danger threatened.

The sight that greeted his eyes froze him in his tracks.

His eyes were immediately drawn to the monster. It was immense. Great spines jutted from its horny carapace of skin. Its long, thin tail whipped the air. It seemed like a creature made all of bone and muscle. It was taller than Darkmane and heavier, and it carried about it an aura of palpable menace that would have made a lesser man shudder. Its eyes were yellow and jaundiced, the pupils a glowing red. Saliva dripped from dagger-length fangs. It menaced its prey with claws longer than a man's hand and sharper than needles.

It loomed over two figures. One was the corpse of a male Elf. It was instantly obvious to Darkmane that he had died heroically: his sword lay in the dirt near his recumbent form. Beside him was a kneeling Elf girl, her hands covered in blood. She looked up at the monster, apparently hypnotized by terror. The creature hissed at her. The sound was eerily like that of a great snake, but what was more terrifying was that there was the suggestion of words, of a language, in the noise it made. The girl whimpered.

'Hold, creature!' shouted Darkmane. 'Leave her alone!'

The Shapechanger turned and gazed at Darkmane quizzically. Its movements were swift and disjointed, like those of a marionette on the end of its strings. There was a suggestion of intelligence in the eyes, an inhuman sentience that regarded the man mockingly. Its appearance reminded Darkmane of the creature he had fought in Drystone, but there was something subtly different

about this one. It moved in a different way, stood in a different posture. Then Darkmane had no more time to ponder about anything. The creature sprang on him.

It made no sound at all, save for the clicking of its joints. Darkmane leapt backwards, ducking below the swing of a razor-edged claw that came so close it shaved off a lock of his hair. Darkmane lashed out with a counter-blow — but the creature was fast, faster than the thing Darkmane had fought in the besieged hall, perhaps even faster than Darkmane himself — and his swing missed.

They exchanged a flurry of blows that were almost too swift for the eye to follow. When they sprang apart again, Darkmane was bleeding from a deep cut in his cheek and the creature had two spines shorn off its back. To Darkmane's horror, the thing now began to change even while he watched. The spines retracted and the carapace grew thicker and hornier, like the hide of a Rhino Man. The beast was now heavily armoured. The two combatants began to circle. Darkmane hoped that Yaztromo would arrive soon.

Behind him, he heard the Elf woman whimpering softly. She was rooted to the spot by fear, and now her fate depended on the outcome of this battle. The monster had retracted the claws of its right hand and clenched it into a fist. As Darkmane watched, the hand seemed to melt and run, remoulding itself into a new shape. When the process was complete, the creature had a studded mace at the end of its arm instead of a hand. Darkmane continued to hold its weird gaze, searching its eyes for a clue to when it would attack.

The thing strode closer, its mace-arm sweeping down in a great arc. It was too late to step aside. Darkmane reached up with his free hand and caught its wrist. The

creature was incredibly strong — but so was Darkmane.
They stood, limbs locked for a second. Darkmane was
forced to drop his sword and grapple with the creature.
At such close quarters he could not use his weapon and
he badly needed to immobilize the creature's other,
taloned hand.

They stood, wrestling, for long moments. Darkmane's
muscles screamed from the effort of holding the creature.
His legs were braced solidly and his feet seemed rooted
to the earth as firmly as a tree. The muscles of his neck
were taut wires and the veins stood out on his forehead.
Darkmane shook his head to shake away the sweat
which rolled down his face, its salt stinging his open
wound. Slowly his coiled strength began to tell and he
began to force the monster back. He saw fear flash
across the creature's red eyes. Then he recoiled in pain as
something sharp slashed his arm and sent him reeling —
he had forgotten about the creature's tail. As he fought
to regain his balance, the creature's mace-hand crashed
down on his shoulder, knocking him to the ground.

The pain in his left arm was so great that he almost
blacked out. Even as he fought to retain consciousness,
Darkmane was aware that it was hopeless. He was
unable to move, a sitting target for the thing's attacks.
Even so, he tried to rise. The creature hissed triumphantly
and its claws slashed at his exposed neck.

'Look out!' the woman screamed.

Darkmane tried to throw himself aside. Even as he did
so, a dark shadow passed by overhead with a flurry of
wings and a great cawing. He rolled along the ground to
where the Elf's sword lay, and snatched it up.

Vermithrax hovered round the monster's head; he
buffeted it ineffectually with his wings and pecked at its
eyes, obscuring the Shapechanger's vision and distracting

its attention from the injured Darkmane. Even as he watched, the bony ridges over the monster's eyebrows extended so that its eyes seemed like glowing fires deep within a cave. It had protected itself from the bird's only effective method of attack. Able to concentrate now without fear of losing an eye, it lashed out with its claw, nearly catching the shrieking bird. Vermithrax flapped skywards out of harm's way.

At the glade's entrance Darkmane caught sight of Yaztromo and Weasel. The wizard stood, wheezing and trying to catch his breath. The little con-man lurked behind the wizard, making ineffective cuts in the air with his knife, despite the fact that the monster was at least ten metres away. It was obviously going to be some time before Yaztromo could enter the fray and, if the creature thought to attack him now, he would prove easy prey. Darkmane knew that Weasel could not stop it. It was up to him. Good! He owed the thing a few wounds.

With renewed determination he closed the gap between himself and the shape-shifter. It took all his willpower to ignore the pain in his shoulder. The creature had looked away from him in order to take in the new arrivals, but now it shifted its full attention back to Darkmane; it reached out with both arms as if trying to embrace him. Its right hand had grown talons again. Darkmane made no effort to avoid the thing. Instead, he dived forward, within the sweep of its embrace, and drove his sword into its stomach with all the force he could muster. The creature hissed as the air was knocked out of it.

Darkmane knelt and moved into a backward roll under its claws. The creature staggered back, the Elvish blade still firmly fixed in its stomach. As it reeled away,

Darkmane saw that the tip of the blade had passed right through it and emerged from its back.

He ran over to where he had dropped his own sword and snatched it up. With a few swift strokes he put the creature out of its agony. Only when the thing was completely still did Weasel run across and begin to hack at the body with his knife.

'Now, monster, you must face the blade of Weasel,' he cried. 'Your doom is assured, for there is no deadlier warrior in all of Allansia!'

'My name is Star,' said the woman, smiling. The reason for her name was obvious to anyone who gazed upon the star-shaped birthmark in the centre of her forehead. 'You have saved my life and I am very much in your debt. If there is any way in which I can repay you, you have but to ask.'

She showed no sign of her earlier fear. Now her every movement spoke of an inner grace and calm. Darkmane examined her closely for the first time. Like all Elves, she was tall and willowy, graceful as a reed swaying in the wind. She was slim and agile, with long, slender legs so that she was only slightly shorter than he. Her face was triangular, her wide, star-marked brow tapering down to a narrow chin. Her ears were pointed, her mouth broad and oddly sensuous.

It was her eyes, though, which dominated her face. They were huge with long, fine lashes. Each iris was of a different colour: one a warm, deep brown, the other a cold, challenging blue. It was a strange face, inhuman almost — but then Elves had always been a race apart. He had to admit that she was beautiful, if in an unnervingly exotic manner.

'I am Chadda Darkmane, a captain in the service of

Salamonis. You owe me no thanks. In rescuing you I have increased my Amonour; that is reward enough.'

Star ran her tongue over her lips. 'I am pleased to have been of some service,' she said with an ironic smile.

'What happened here?' asked Darkmane gruffly. He was pleased to hear Yaztromo and Weasel approaching. The girl's cool glance was strangely disturbing. 'Why did the monster attack you and your companion? How do you come to be in this place?'

'One question at a time, my handsome friend,' she said, still smiling and holding his gaze. 'Celanion and I came here seeking the medicinal roots that are said to grow in this part of the forest.'

'Indeed they do, fair lady,' said Weasel. He grabbed her hand in his and began to kiss it in a parody of courtliness. 'If I can be of any help to you in your quest, please let me know. I am Weasel, and I am as great a lover as I am a warrior. And my swordsmanship is famed throughout Allansia, you know what I mean?'

Star snatched her hand away as if she had touched something disgusting and slimy. Before she could speak, however, Yaztromo chimed in.

'What roots would these be? I have never heard of any medicinal plants growing here, and I am considered something of an authority on these matters.'

'I know not. Celanion was the herbalist. I was merely his companion.'

'And I'm sure you were a fine companion at that,' said Weasel in an oily tone. He moved closer to the Elf woman and laid his arm across her shoulder, rather too familiarly, Darkmane thought. 'You must be distraught at his loss. If you require someone to comfort you, well, I can state in all humility that I've had plenty of experience at comforting distraught maidens.'

Star broke away from his grasp and moved nearer Darkmane. She stood so close, he believed he could feel the warmth of her body. 'Who is your venerable companion?' she asked, glancing at the wizard.

'I am Yaztromo of Darkwood.' The sorcerer ran his fingers through his beard. He stood proudly erect, as if awaiting his due recognition. Star just stared at him as if she'd never heard of the famous mage. Yaztromo scowled. 'You haven't answered my questions, girl! Why did the monster attack you?'

'I know not. It all happened so suddenly. We've never had any trouble before, but things have changed since the old Hellsgate Keep gained its new occupants.'

'Hellsgate? Why, that is where we are bound!' Weasel piped up.

Darkmane shot him a warning glance as sharp as any dagger. 'What do you know of the Keep's master?' he asked to cover the guide's blunder.

'Almost nothing, save that Orcs, Goblins and worse have flocked to the area. We have seen strange lights silhouetting the fortress against the night sky and have heard rumours of evil sorcery. If you seek Hellsgate, then you must be a hero, for only a hero would venture there now. We left the area as soon as we saw how things were there.'

'You know the way there?' asked Darkmane, taking no notice of Yaztromo who was deliberately shaking his head.

'Yes, of course. Do you wish me to guide you? 'Tis a dark path but I would risk it if you desire to go. It is the least service I could do for one who has saved my life.'

Darkmane considered. He did not want any more strangers knowing what they were about, and he was loath to lead someone so recently rescued into certain peril. On the other hand, Weasel was obviously not to be trusted as a guide, and besides, there was something intriguing about Star.

Darkmane came to a decision. 'All right. If you are willing to take us, then you shall be our guide.'

She reached out and clasped his hand as merchants do to seal a bargain. 'I would take you anywhere,' she muttered.

'Ahem!' coughed Yaztromo. 'Don't you think we should bury your late companion?'

Star nodded. 'Yes, I suppose we'd better.'

11

Tell Us the Secret

Staring down on Axion's recumbent form, Cawlis permitted himself a satisfied smile. Everything was going according to plan. Through the power of the Bloodstone, the Great Magus was incarnate once more. Soon he would reveal the knowledge that Cawlis and his masters so desperately needed to know.

Look at you, he thought. *You're not so much now, are you? Just a sack of flesh animated by sorcery and the power stored up in those old relics. To think that once kingdoms scuttled to obey your every whim and the lives of frantic thousands were ordered by your whispered commands. I could almost feel pity for you. If pity were an emotion of which I was capable.*

Axion lay on the rune-decorated slab once more, as he had for the past two days. His brief surge of energy at the end of the ritual had proved only temporary, and he had lapsed back into a state of dormancy. Cawlis knew that it would take the Great Magus some time to accustom himself to his new form, now that he had returned from whichever realms he had been wandering in these past millennia. This was to be expected; it was all in the plan.

Tell Us the Secret

Cawlis ran his fingers over the Great Magus's translucent skin, admiring his own handiwork. The pinkish muscles looked atrophied, but they would soon gain strength. His skeletal structure was sound. The writhing maggots had already formed part of a digestive system. The Bloodstone pulsed warmly within the chest cavity, each magical heartbeat fitfully illuminating the chamber and Axion's internal structure. All in all, things were going splendidly. It was almost time to move on to the next stage.

Cawlis stroked his chin and struggled to contain his feeling of exaltation. He had an overwhelming urge to gloat. This was the peril of maintaining a single form for so long; one started to take on the characteristics of the being one was impersonating. He knew that if he stayed human for much longer he would be corrupted by their emotionality and their limited perceptions. *Ah, but would that be so bad?* part of his mind enquired. Would he be able to enjoy his coming triumph so well in any other form? Almost of their own accord, his lips twisted into a smile.

The Shapechanger clapped his hands. Axion opened his jewelled eyes. The light of the Bloodstone burned within them. His eye-sockets resembled pits of volcanic lava. The illumination from within turned his face into a demon mask.

'So weak,' he said softly, the multiple voices echoing round the chamber, oddly counterpointing the wheezing of his part-formed lungs. 'I dreamed, you know, Abrascia; I dreamed my keep was invaded, and intruders overcame me and destroyed my physical form. I retreated. I retreated to the heart of the Bloodstone and it was worse than any death . . . I dreamed I was summoned back by a monster that wore the shape of a man.'

Cawlis wondered who the Great Mage thought he was talking to. Hadn't Abrascia been the name of his consort?

Axion made to rise. It was a tentative movement, reminiscent of a child's first attempt to walk or the faltering movements of a dying man. 'So weak, Abrascia. My strength has been stolen and my body feels strange . . . the pain so great. What nightmare is this?'

'No nightmare, Dread Lord,' said Cawlis ingratiatingly. 'You were overcome by the treachery of your enemies. Your spirit retreated within the Stone of Blood. But I have brought you back . . . I have rejoined your scattered parts. I have recalled your sundered spirit to this world. I have brought you back to complete your mission.'

'You should not have.' In the course of a single sentence the voices magnified from a whisper to a scream, to a roar, then back to an entreaty. 'Not a dream? Then I have no mission. I failed . . . the fools, I tried to give them life eternal. I tried to overcome Death himself and restore to man his stolen immortality. They turned against me, then? It was to be expected I suppose. The gods are jealous and men are fools.'

'You did not fail, Dread Lord. You created life. You tore its secrets from the wombs of mothers. Your creations conquered an Empire for you. You and your followers lived for centuries.' Cawlis's voice fell to a whisper. 'You must share your secrets with me. You must tell me everything.'

'I cannot remember. I have forgotten so much while I was dreaming my long dream of unlife. Let me return to whither I came from, or kill me. It would be the only mercy.'

'Alas, those are things I cannot do, Lord Axion. You must share your secrets with me. I can permit nothing less. Tell me of the process you used to create your slave races. Tell me how you would have overcome Death. I seek to continue your great work.'

'Death cannot be overcome! He can only be cheated temporarily. I thought I could learn the ultimate secrets of the cosmos. Hah! The universe is as it is and cannot be changed. I killed all those innocents in my experiments . . . and that is what I learned. And you think I would tell you my secrets so that you may repeat my folly! Even if I could remember them, I would not tell you.'

It was as Cawlis had feared. Axion's long unlife had left him deranged. Worse, he had lost memories. Well, that would return when his body was restored to full strength.

'I would tell you nothing! Nothing!' The multiple voices shouted and screamed, entwined in one another.

'Oh but you will, Dread Lord. Believe me, you will. I have repaired your old chambers. Even as we speak they are being prepared for your coming. I will grant you life and in exchange you will grant me power.'

'NOOO! Let me die!' Even Cawlis shuddered at the sound of the sorcerer's many voices as they pleaded with him. Yes, he thought, he had definitely worn this form too long if he was now starting to experience fear.

The Troll waited in his master's chambers. He was nervous, though he knew he shouldn't be. He had performed his mission more than adequately and had returned with many new bodies for Cawlis's experiments. This audience-chamber would make a Demon from the depths of all the hells nervous, he thought in his slow and ponderous way. Whoever had designed it knew how to inspire fear. It was as cold as the heart of a necromancer. Breath emerged in clouds that joined the mists covering the floor. When the Troll clapped his hands together to keep them warm, the sound echoed away to infinity. There were times when the Troll thought he ought not to make any noise, that any noise he did make would attract the unwelcome attentions of something dark and hungry . . .

The lower chambers of Hellsgate Keep had been carved out of the cold grey rock of the Moonstone Hills according to a very peculiar pattern. It was as if the builders had sought to copy the internal structure of a living thing. The arches that supported the ceilings reminded the Troll of ribs. Here and there, spikes protruded from the walls like the quills of a porcupine. From the stone spears dangled the impaled bodies of victims. Brown trails marred the walls beneath the bodies, where blood had caked and hardened.

In front of him was Cawlis's throne: a giant piece of ebon wood carved into the shape of some crouching, alien beast. It resembled one of the wilder shapes the Troll had seen his master adopt in combat. The throne sat in the middle of the strange pattern of channels that grooved the floor. The Troll had known times when these channels ran crimson with the lifeblood of his victims. The stuff streamed into the conduit below the throne and bubbled down to only Cawlis knew where. Sometimes the Troll wondered what his master was really up to, but he knew enough to keep his own counsel. In his experience, sorcerers were apt to get annoyed if questioned as to their purpose. He fingered his lucky locket nervously.

Suddenly Lord Cawlis was there, standing directly in front of him. The Troll wondered whether he had entered the room so silently that he hadn't noticed, or had he simply materialized out of thin air? He wouldn't put that beyond his master's abilities. It took him several uncomfortable moments to regain control of his faculties and make his report.

'Things went well, master. Twenty new bodies for your spell-rooms.'

Cawlis seemed distracted: a frown marred his smooth white brow and his saturnine features were grim. 'Yes, yes. Good work. Have the bodies taken down to the letting room. Their vital juices will give our guest his strength back. Let us hope they improve his memory.'

The Troll stood, nonplussed, wondering what his master was talking about. Was he expected to make a reply?

'What are you waiting for? Be about your business,' said Cawlis mildly.

The Troll hurried away. He found the Shapechanger's quietly polite voice more frightening than the battle-cry of a hundred warriors.

In the frigid corridors beneath the keep, cries rang out. They were uttered by five voices that seemed somehow intermingled, so that they said the same words over and over again, sometimes as a plea, sometimes as an order. On occasions another voice would reply, mild, polite and diffident, but with something about it that suggested mockery. Even those black-hearted creatures that lurked in the shadowy passages quaked when they heard that voice, for there was something inhuman and agelessly cruel about it. The voices echoed down the great maze of corridors and drifted down like mists into the night-black depths beneath the fortress.

In the lesser depths the Groan, eyeless monsters white as bone, threw themselves on their slimy bellies and offered prayers to their bat-winged god for deliverance.

Shadowmaster

The sound of their prayers reached the ears of the aged priest of the Forgotten Lord who tolled his warning bell. For half a century, like his father before him, he had sat in the darkness waiting for the sign. He was proud to be the one chosen to give it. No sooner had the bell's leaden tolling faded than his heart stopped beating and he died.

The great spider which the Dwarfs had called Krya-Shebboth ceased spinning her webs over the Drop when the echoes reached her, for she understood the words and knew what would happen when the five voices ceased to oppose the one. She picked up the Goblin corpse in her envenomed mandibles and scuttled to her larder. She knew when it was time to seek shelter.

Further, deeper still, those whose true names are for ever hidden from the world picked up the pattern of vibrations in the ether, and something akin to joy stirred in their fathomless minds. Perhaps soon they would be called upon to feed.

Across the nighted depths of the Brightloam Caverns all manner of creatures, masters and servants, waited breathlessly. Waiting for whatever would come next.

Axion raised his head and gazed around with burning eyes. He was upright now, a puppet dangling in a web of vein-like pipes. He could hear the gurgling of obscene fluids within them and feel aches from the areas where the tubes entered his body. He was still weak, and the tubes were the only things that kept him upright.

He had been dreaming again; dreaming of that other place, beyond hurt, beyond pain. He had paced through a gloomy castle, through corridors laced by cobwebs. He had looked on mildewed pictures that had shown himself as a youth: proud, finely clad, murderous and powerful,

feared and loved and hated. The pictures had shown him before his experiments had altered his body. Afterwards, no artist could bear to look upon his form. He had smelled the rotten hangings and the salty, moist air and had listened to the wild, discordant music of untuned harps coming from the great ballroom in which, he knew, skeletons danced.

The music was mocking and the bodies belonged to old friends and enemies long since dead. They were the unclothed bones of lovers and children and servants. They had known him in another time when he had worn his rightful body, not this unholy abomination.

No! He did not want to think about that, to think of what was happening to him. Better to recollect the dream. Best of all to recall turning and fleeing the castle and then suddenly not to be in the corridors any longer but in the quiet, restful graveyard, sitting on the tumbled headstone of some forgotten merchant, looking at the angel-winged statue that guarded the mausoleum of his consort, Abrascia. It had been peaceful there, utterly quiet. Everything had been muffled in a drifting grey mist that obscured its harsher outlines. The graveyard had been real, he told himself. More real than this place. It was within the realm of the Bloodstone where his spirit had rested and rotted for centuries. That was his true home, not here, suspended above this cauldron of blood, bound by dark magic while a mocking captor, who pretended to be a servant, looked on.

The Bloodstone had held his disembodied spirit. It had provided him with a place for dreams, a refuge where he controlled his surroundings, where what he imagined came true. He needed to go back there. All he had to do was die. The spell that bound him to the gem would suck him back there permanently at the moment of his last heartbeat. Then he would be safe.

Tell Us the Secret

He tried not to remember what had happened next in the graveyard: of the way the bony fingers had erupted from the earth to clutch at his ankles, of the way the skeletons had drawn themselves forth from their grave to stand, gleaming by the light of the full moon. He did not want to contemplate what such dreams might mean. He wanted only to be free.

He tried to rock himself back and forth within the web of cables, to pull himself free of the terrible tendrils that fed him nutrients and kept him tied to this dreadful place. The tubes swayed with his body but did not give way.

'It is no use, lord,' came the mocking voice of his tormentor. 'You will have to be much stronger than that to snap those feed pipes. Fortunately, that is just what they are making you. They pipe the vital juices of lesser mortals into you, restoring your body to full and vital health. It will need to be healthy to . . . but no, there will be time enough to discuss my plans later. May I tell you how well you look? Perhaps you would like to see for yourself. Open your eyes!'

Axion found himself unable to resist the command. Were the nutrients that were being pumped in laden with some will-deadening drug? He knew of several that might be used. He had also once known ways to fight them, if only he could remember. He had forgotten so much in the Bloodstone's realm. He had needed to remember so little.

Slowly his eyes opened and he found himself staring into the silvered glass of a Dwarf-made mirror. The figure he saw was a fleshless horror with a glowing heart, a monster from the worst nightmares of his childhood. It was himself. He wanted to scream but wouldn't. He refused to give his captor the satisfaction.

'Isn't it nice to know that your experiment in immortality worked? There was more than enough of you left to remake you. Your experiments succeeded.'

Images flickered through Axion's mind, scenes from the time when he had experimented on living beings, hoping to plumb the secrets of life and death. He saw the faces of his victims: young men and women who screamed as vital glands were taken from their bodies while they still lived. He saw the grotesque, mis-shapen creatures that at first had flopped forth from his vats and tried to take their own lives. He saw the bloated, purple bodies of the victims of the plague he had accidentally unleashed, part of an experiment in controlling virulent diseases. He saw his mistakes and his follies and his cruelties. He had forgotten them over the centuries, and now they were flooding back.

'You don't understand!' he pleaded, listening to the distorted voices that issued from his body. 'I failed. I took the wrong path. My work was madness. When I started I was young and proud and foolish. When I was older I was too vain to admit my mistakes. I unleashed plagues and monsters. My experiments led only to deformities. I could not improve on life.'

Cawlis grinned. 'You created so many new things, Dread Lord, wonderful things. Like Shapechangers, for instance. Like me.'

For the first time Axion looked at the creature with unclouded eyes. He saw the strangeness of the thing, the subtle differences from his old creations. Could they have changed so much during the time of his undeath, or was this something else entirely? 'You are no true Shapechanger. You've worn that body too long in my presence. I see you prefer it to your own form. You are corrupted.'

Tell Us the Secret

'I prefer to say "changed", lord, merely "changed".'

Hearing the mockery in the thing's voice made Axion determined to free himself. To do that, he would need his old knowledge. He must remember more. It did not occur to him to ask himself why his captor had begun to smile.

12

The Hellsgate

From the cliff's edge Darkmane watched the stream tumble and splash along the ravine-bottom, far, far below. From this height, he thought, the place was quite beautiful. The swirling water turned white with turbulence where it encountered rocks. Huge boulders jutted out into the stream, partially obstructing the flow. Where the water tumbled down into small pools, a fine mist made rainbows leap into view. On the opposite side of the ravine, the cliffs rose ever higher, a mighty jumble of rock at the top of which, Darkmane knew, stood the Hellsgate. At present it was hidden from view by the folds of the hills. Everything looked peaceful. Even the chill gave the air a clean tang. The wind's bite brought colour to a man's cheeks and made him feel glad to be alive.

It was in places like this, the wild, remote spots far from the haunts of men, that Darkmane felt most happy. He enjoyed the isolation and the peace. If only the sorcerer and his monstrous followers had not chosen this place for their lair. For a moment he thought he could be quite happy, building a little cabin down by the stream and living there with the right person. He eyed Star thoughtfully.

She, too, was lost in reverie; she stared at the rock-face beside the pool as if searching for a half-remembered landmark. As if sensing Darkmane's eyes upon her, she turned and smiled at him. She was a strange one, Darkmane thought. Her face was gaunt and pale. For the past two days she had eaten nothing, insisting that she was maintaining a mourning fast for her dead companion. She had refused all offers to share their meagre supplies until the companions began to feel rude importuning her and gave up their efforts. Now she looked gaunt, her high cheekbones clearly visible through her flawless skin. There was no denying her beauty, though.

Weasel clearly thought so, too. He stood, gazing raptly at her. Every now and again he would lick his lips.

Darkmane did not smile back, and she looked away, eyes downcast. Darkmane cursed himself. He did not mean to be rude; it was just that she brought out the gruff side of his personality.

'Where is the entrance to the Brightloam Caverns, girl?' he asked, wondering why he couldn't bring himself to produce his customary politeness towards women.

She pointed down to the rock-face beside the largest pool. 'Beyond that bend, just out of view.'

'And how do we get down, my pretty one?' asked Weasel, sidling up and touching her arm as if to get her attention. 'Perhaps you and I should go off alone and scout.'

Star pulled a face and moved away from Weasel, closer to the cliff edge. Weasel thought twice about following.

'There is a path here,' she said, indicating the cliff edge. With the surefootedness of a mountain cat,

Darkmane moved over to stand beside her. He noticed how the wind whipped her hair, moving a lock away from her pointed ear, and how gracefully she smoothed it back into place. Slowly he dragged his attention away from her.

There was indeed a path down the side of the ravine where she indicated. It was narrow, perhaps as wide as the span from Darkmane's fingertips to his elbow, and it seemed worn smooth by the passage of many feet. It traced its way down and eventually reached the ravine floor, all that dizzying distance below.

'This is where our ways part, girl,' he said.

'No . . . I . . . I wish to go with you.'

'You cannot,' Yaztromo said from behind them. 'It is far too dangerous. We would not risk your life now. You have been a fair guide to us, and now you have done your part. You have our eternal gratitude.'

Was it just his imagination, Darkmane wondered, or did the wizard seem grateful for the excuse to send Star on her way? Not that it mattered; the sorcerer was correct. Intrigued as he was by the Elvish girl, Darkmane could not countenance putting her life at risk – even if it meant saying goodbye to her here.

'Yaztromo is right,' he said. He looked meaningfully at Weasel. 'You have led us well, unlike some I could name, and you have repaid the debt you felt you owed us for your life. I would not wish to see you indebted to us again.'

She walked over to him boldly and looked him directly in the eye. Darkmane felt his face flush with unaccustomed embarrassment. 'I do believe you want rid of me, Sir Darkmane.' She twirled gracefully, her cloak fluttering in the wind. 'Am I so unpleasing to you?'

'No . . .'

The Hellsgate

'You cannot go below, Star,' said Yaztromo, and Darkmane was grateful for his intervention. 'We must face dreadful foes and this is work for adventurers, not for maidens. I forbid you to accompany us and that is final.'

Star looked as if she was going to pout, but then she turned and walked away. She held her head high and did not look back. Darkmane was sorry to have offended her and regretted having parted on such poor terms, but part of him was also definitely relieved to see her go.

'Now that is one sweet maiden whose company I'd like to keep,' Weasel leered suggestively. 'I've half a mind to go after her.'

'C-rawk! Why don't you? Half a mind is all you've got to offer!' jibed Vermithrax, who had become more than a little annoyed by Weasel's culinary suggestions for the crow.

'Because your masters still owe me money. Because those raiders have looted many villages, and who knows what treasure they may have? And because there are always tasty maidens queuing up for a man like me, you know what I mean? Back home I've got to beat them off with a stick. You know, there was once this princess . . . Heck, what am I doing telling stories to a crow?'

Now that Star had gone, Yaztromo was gazing fixedly at the cliff opposite. His face had a remote, abstracted look to it, as if he were concentrating very hard on listening to some distant sound. A frown passed across his wrinkled brow and he shook his head slightly.

Darkmane tore himself from thoughts of the departed Star. 'What is it, Gereth? What troubles you?'

'Nothing I can put a finger on, but I sense great danger.' Leaning heavily on his staff, the old man led them on to the narrow path. Vermithrax sprang from his

shoulder and spread his wings to catch the up-draught from the cliff edge. Slowly he drifted upwards, a smudge of dark shadow outlined against the cold blue sky.

Slowly and ever so carefully, they edged away from the sun's light. It was dark and cool in the tunnel, and the air was damp and fusty. Above them a torch flickered; they were set every fifty paces, a sign that these depths were definitely inhabited and these tunnels regularly used. Star's information had been right: they had found the cave entrance to the tunnels just beyond the pool. The way underneath the cliffs had proven surprisingly accessible. It had all been a little too easy, Darkmane thought uneasily. He felt the enormous weight of the cliff-face above bearing down on him. Darkmane prided himself on the fact that

The Hellsgate

he feared nothing save
dishonour, but this shad-
owy darkness and the en-
closed space made him
distinctly uneasy.

Weasel fumbled inside
a sack, then from within
he produced a small clay
pot. Pulling out the stop-
per, he extracted the
body of a dead bat.

'What are you doing?'
Darkmane asked. He
spoke softly, knowing
that a whisper would
carry further in these
quiet depths than the
normal tones of his con-
versation.

Weasel slit the bat's
throat and began to daub
his face with its blood.
'Bat's blood,' he whis-
pered loudly. 'It'll let me
see in the dark.'

'Nonsense,' Darkmane
hissed. 'There's no magic
to bat's blood. What do
you say, Yaztromo?'

Yaztromo stood stock
still, his face ashen. His
knuckles were white
where they gripped his
staff so tightly.

'I sense it,' he said eventually. 'I feel the same dark presence I felt at Drystone. He, or it, is here. Something terrible is going to happen.'

From ahead of them came the sound of guttural voices. Orcs! Darkmane gestured for the others to be silent. Soft-footed, the three adventurers padded forward, cat-quiet and wary. Backs to the wall, they edged as far as the bend in the tunnel and risked a glance round it.

Darkmane's heart fell at what he saw. The tunnel suddenly stopped at a deep ravine that cut into the depths of the ancient rock. The yawning abyss was far too wide for even a man of his mighty strength to risk a leap. On the far side, beneath a weirdly carved stone arch, two Orcs manned an extending drawbridge contraption. It was obvious now how regular visitors entered the Brightloam Caverns. Darkmane doubted whether the watchmen would extend the bridge for him, no matter how politely he asked.

Backing away, he signalled for the others to follow him back down the tunnel.

The sunlight momentarily blinded Darkmane as he emerged from the caves once more. He squinted, giving his eyes time to adjust. Spray from the pool flecked his face. Weasel bumped into his back and rebounded.

'What now?' asked Darkmane. 'We can't go through that way.'

'Maybe you should just pay me my money and go home,' suggested Weasel.

'Perhaps I could be of help,' said a familiar voice. Darkmane wheeled, wrenching his sword from its scabbard. Lying on the top of a nearby rock was Star. Spray had plastered her clothing to her body.

The Hellsgate

'I thought you might have some problems,' she said. 'So I decided to wait here and see if you reappeared.'

Darkmane glanced up at the sheer face of the cliff. 'How do we get up there? We need wings!'

'Yes. Let's just grow them, eh?' said Weasel. 'Then we could flap our way to the top.'

'So you want to go up there, handsome warrior? I may just have the solution to your problem. Follow me!'

Obscurely glad to see her again, Darkmane followed. Licking his lips with a wet, smacking sound, Weasel did the same. Only the troubled Yaztromo stared warily after the girl. He extended his arm. From high above, Vermithrax dropped like a stone and landed on his wrist.

13

Elumbar

'What strangeness is this?' Darkmane enquired, glaring at the brightly painted rocks. They were covered in all manner of bizarre patterns and signs.

'I don't recognize any of these runes,' said Yaztromo in his most portentous manner. 'Nor do I sense any residue of magical energy.'

Star smiled. 'These are Elumbar's works of art. He sometimes comes here and paints the rocks when he's had too much mushroom wine.'

'Does he paint the trees as well?' asked Weasel, pointing at an ancient oak standing on the lake side. Its branches had been splashed with azure paint and the trunk was a swirling mess, painted with all the colours of the rainbow.

'It would seem so,' said Star dryly. 'He's something of a character; he's an acquaintance of Celanion's rather than of mine. I only met him once.'

The number of oddly painted trees increased as they followed the path away from the lake. Here and there they came upon rocks that had been roughly carved into the crude likenesses of men and beasts. They were caught like spirits half-emerging from the stone. It was as if the would-be sculptor had grown bored and had given up each creation half-way through carving it. Many of the incomplete statues were also splashed with paint. One bore the painted paw-prints of an animal. If Darkmane had not known better, he could have sworn that someone had dipped a cat's paws in paint then made it walk over the stone. He dismissed the thought as illogical.

They found the house in the glade. It was the strangest building Darkmane had ever seen: a ramshackle structure, made of wood, to which several entirely new levels seemed to have been added only as an afterthought. Carved verandahs emerged from its sides; some were nowhere near any doors or windows. The entrance on the ground floor had been boarded up, and the new one was reached by a rickety flight of stairs leading to the third storey. A carved horse, twice as tall as a man, supported these stairs. One whole section of wall had been ripped away on the second floor, exposing the room inside to the elements. The various parts of the building were all painted in violently clashing colours. Just looking at its chaos made Darkmane feel ill.

In the clearing in front of the house sat an Elf. He took the mouthpiece of a water pipe away from his cat and inhaled deeply himself. He fluttered some fingers at Star by way of greeting, took a swig from a wine flask, offered some to the cat, then took another swig himself.

'Come on, Cat, you've got to take some sooner or later. I don't like drinking on my own.' For the first time the Elf seemed to notice that he had visitors and lurched to his feet. He wandered across to greet them, looking none too steady.

As he approached, Darkmane could see that Elumbar was dressed peculiarly, even for an Elf. He wore a long robe woven from thread of a great many colours and belted at the waist with a silk sash. His hair was as long as Star's and just as fine, and his eyes were obscured by pink-lensed spectacles. Many rings covered his fingers, and his feet were bare. Darkmane noticed that painted cat's paw-prints were traced over part of his outlandish coat.

Elumbar shook his head. 'Cat won't drink with me. He's feeling a bit temperamental today. Hey! Star, like good to see you. How's Celanion? Still mellow?'

'He's dead.'

'That's not good. Well, maybe it was time for him to try something new anyway. Fate, lady, who can outrun it? Ah, and who are these lovely people?'

Star introduced her companions, particularly stressing Darkmane's heroism. When she introduced the wizard, Elumbar chuckled.

'Yaztromo of Darkwood, eh? Loved your book, *Herbs of the Western Forest* — a classic, my man. Hey, didn't I buy a potion from you once?'

Yaztromo shuffled his feet in embarrassment. 'Maybe.'

'Potion of levitation — yeah, I remember. Me and Celanion drank it just before Winter Solstice. Hoo, we were really flying after that one. You remember that, Star? Oh no, forgot: you only came with Cel last trip. Oh well, happy days, eh?'

'We hear you're the man to see for a balloon,' Darkmane said, a little too brusquely. Elumbar stopped talking, took off his glasses and polished them, then set them back on the bridge of his nose.

'Sorry, what was that you said?'

'We'd like you to lend us a balloon,' said Yaztromo. 'We have a vital mission . . .'

'A balloon? Why didn't you say so? Sure thing; you've come to the right place.'

He led them round to the back of the house where various baskets and burners and large pieces of patched cloth lay in various stages of manufacture.

'That's a good one,' he said, pointing to a red gas-bag decorated with a painted rose. 'Nice spider-silk bag, hardly ever crashes. I built her for a prince of the southlands; wanted to use her to spy in some war. Told him I couldn't let any of my devices be used to, like, harm people. Or there's Greenblossom. No . . . forget I said that, she needs two more patches . . . I know, this one's just the thing. My latest design, got the idea watching an eagle in flight. Can't improve on nature, right, Star?'

Darkmane looked dubiously at the device. The basket looked fine but there seemed to be too many strange attachments on the uninflated bag. As Elumbar talked, Darkmane noticed that Cat was stalking closer and closer to Vermithrax.

'Yeah, bag's got a lateral wing; improves stability, makes it easier to fly. Well, it should. Haven't really tried it yet. Don't worry though, it's a classic.'

Cat pounced on Vermithrax. There was a brief struggle and much yowling and cawing. The next thing everyone knew, Cat was fleeing. He bounded past Darkmane and leapt into Elumbar's arms. Effortlessly Elumbar caught him and began to stroke his fur absent-mindedly.

'Tell you what, why don't you lovely people stay for the night, and in the morning we'll see what we can do for you. I'm a little bit under the weather at the moment, to tell you the truth.'

Ever since he'd first met this Elumbar, Darkmane had become increasingly dubious. This adventure seemed to be cursed with incompetents, and things were going wrong at every turn. It had been bad enough hiring Weasel as a guide; Darkmane was in no hurry to compound his error by hiring this degenerate as a balloon-maker, even if Star did recommend him. On the other hand, though, it was getting late and it would be nice to sleep under a roof again, even one as gaudily painted as this one.

'Master Elumbar, we'd love to stay,' said Yaztromo, taking the matter out of his hands.

14

Cheating Death

'Before I died, what I desired most was immortality. Ironic, is it not?' Axion's strange voice was stronger now. It resonated with some of its old assurance.

'You did not die, lord,' Cawlis corrected him gently. 'You merely rested for centuries. Those ignorant fools could not end your great work. Your spirit triumphed over death. After all, I brought you back.'

Cawlis was suspicious. Even allowing for the mind-controlling enchantments and the wit-addling drugs that had been pumped into his body through the umbilical pipes, the aged sorcerer had been too co-operative. The Shapechanger looked up at the skeletal form of the once-mighty wizard and met his burning, bejewelled gaze. The nutrient fluids were doing their job, of that there could be no doubt. Axion had more flesh and more muscle mass. Every so often he twitched, sending ripples up the strands that supported his healing body.

Axion's echoing laughter rang out. There was something fundamentally unstable about him, Cawlis decided. The centuries he had inhabited the Bloodstone had driven him mad. Being without body for so long would do that to any mortal. There were times when Axion seemed to take a hellish pleasure in imparting his dark secrets, and there were others when he was so depressed that he was paralysed with doubt. Still, no matter; the task was well under way. The host bodies were maturing.

'Yesss! You brought me back.' Was there a trace of bitterness, of hate even, in Axion's voice? 'A mighty feat of sorcery and one which I could not have performed better myself. I did that too, you know – summoned up the spirits of the dead to enquire what lay beyond the grave. Poor wraiths; they were but shadows of their mortal selves and could give no meaningful answers. They struggled against my binding spells, seeking to leech the life from my body. In the end I dismissed them and was no wiser.'

Axion's eyes dimmed. The Bloodstone in his chest pulsed less brightly. It was now almost completely hidden by the thickening flesh, visible only as a dim glow of balefire suffusing the area where the mage's heart should have been.

'But you did succeed, Dread Lord. You mastered the creation of new life and the secrets of eluding death. You have proved both these things to me. What you have never revealed to me is how.'

Axion's eyelids drooped and the fire of his eyes was completely extinguished. His head slumped forward as if in defeat.

'How? How? By dint of lifetimes of effort and the suffering of guiltless thousands,' the voices intoned softly. 'By travelling long leagues and scouring antique libraries. By sailing dark oceans and forcing demons to do my will. Oh, but I was young and vital in those days and gave no thought to cost or consequence. My bride

Cheating Death

and I were going to live for ever, were going to laugh at
the gods and mock old Death himself. Aye, nothing was
going to stop me; let the gods show mercy to the fools
who stood in my way, for I would not . . .'

'You speak in riddles, lord. How did you gain access
to the mysteries of creation? How did you stumble upon
the secret of Haellsgarth?' Axion was being unusually
garrulous and Cawlis chose his words carefully to sustain
the mood for as long as possible.

'I travelled all Allansia, from Carsepolis to the Sea of
Pearls, from the Ice Wastes to the Glimmering Sea. I
talked with master sorcerers and listened to the gibbered
legends of the Ice Ghouls. I read the pictoglyphs of the
Old Civilization in the ruins of time-lost Araniaan. I built
laboratories and experimented on screaming slaves. And
I was still no wiser.

'I scoured graveyards and animated corpses. I heard
rumours of success from many lands and sailed to the
Old World and across the Ocean of Storms to the wild
continent of Khul. Mirages and phantoms all. I wasted
years – nay, decades – in fruitless wanderings till my
hair was grey with age and my bones creaked. Despair
overcame me then, and almost did I forsake my quest,
seeing it as an insane waste of time and effort. And
then . . .'

*In the corridors below the ancient keep they grew. Hanging
from the walls by gossamer webs, the chrysalises began to
pulse with life. The Goblins who watched over them shuddered
as they gazed at the horny carapaces and wondered what
strange new life pulsed within. They looked upon the intricate,
vein-like web of living pipes through which flowed obscene
nutrient fluids, and even the dim, slow minds of the Orcs
were moved to wonder and terror. In the secret recesses of the*

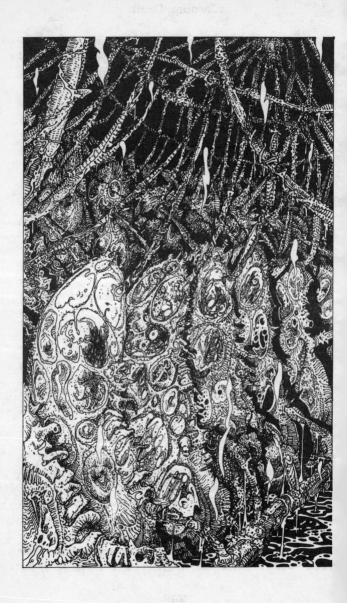

fast-growing masses, the spark of life and alien sentience began to flicker and grow. Soon, so soon.

'. . . And then came my first breakthrough. In an ancient grimoire, so old it pre-dated the War of the Wizards, I found the spell known as Logaan's Secret. It was the work of an ancient cabal of sorcerers known as the Lifters of the Crimson Veil, an organization so secret and feared in their time that, when their enemies overcame them, all records of their very existence were expunged and all traces of their work destroyed lest any who followed might learn their deadly secret. Yes, all traces — save one. How that ancient book survived I know not, but survive it did, until it reached my hands.

'I bought it from a trader who claimed to have found it in the ruins of Goldoran. I had little hope when I purchased it and resolved to roast the peddler over a fire of alchemical flame if he had misled me. But as I flipped through those dust-grimed pages, I knew, I knew! that at last I had found a key. I held the one part of the puzzle that threw new light on all the other parts. I gave the merchant more gold than he could have spent in a lifetime and sent him on his way. Then I set to work.'

Cawlis licked his lips in anticipation. He was so close now to understanding all the mysteries to which Axion alluded. He fought back the suffocating human feeling of glee that filled him. *Do not let the glands and emotions of this form sway you, fool*, he chided himself, but he gloated none the less.

Axion's voices were rising now, full of passion as he recalled the greatest period of his long-interrupted life.

'My first experiments were not a success. They were dead-ends. Oh, I created life: the lurking Thia-kan, the semi-sentient Korgars, the mighty Axaz. All gone now, unsuccessful, could not compete with the creatures that already dwelt in the world. But they were just basic exercises, my apprenticeship really, a prelude to my real artistry. Next came the Shapechangers, an aberrant experiment in transmutation, but an advance. When released, they thrived and took their place in the world full of cunning and cannibal hunger.

'And then came the word I had been waiting for. I captured one of the long-lived Dwarfs of Haellsgarth and, under the influence of certain persuasive if painful implements, I compelled him to reveal to me the secret of their longevity. I found out the secret of the sap that springs from the wells below this keep. In my folly I was convinced that I had found what I was looking for.'

Within the pods, pregnant and pendulous with new life, things stirred and hungered. Bizarre thoughts filled their minds, obscure drives propelled them towards consciousness. The Goblin servitors watching the chrysalises pulse and writhe, imagined monsters waiting to be born. Even fear of their master was not enough to hold them in their place, and they turned and fled.

'I drove the Dwarfs from the deeps and exterminated them, to the last child. I sought the wells of life and drank deep from them. My greying hair grew dark again, my back unbent. I retired to my laboratory near these very chambers and distilled from the waters the essence of immortality – or so I thought! I drank of my potion and my wife did likewise. We sloughed off our old, wrinkled skins like snakes, and new, baby-soft skin was beneath. Our teeth grew firm and we recovered the bright appetites of youth. And so began the days of my invisible empire.'

Cheating Death

'Go on, lord,' Cawlis urged, his voice a hoarse whisper. 'Go on.'

'When word of my discovery became known, kings went down on their bended knee to be my clients, merchants offered the profits of a lifetime for a single sip. I wielded power beyond imagining, for who would not pay with their very soul to regain the lost vitality of their youth? I held a secret beyond price, which many sought to wrest from me. They paid with their lives. My clients paid with their lands and their fortunes.

'Looking back now, I find it hard to comprehend why I did what I did. I was different then, made bitter and ambitious by long years of searching and failure. I wanted glory and recognition and power; I wanted reward for my triumph and obeisance from my fellow men. I received them too. Much good it did me!

'It took the plague several decades to appear and, of course, I was its first victim. For had I not been the first to taste the bitter waters of eternal life? The human body is different in essence from that of the Dwarfs. The waters, which had increased *their* lifespans, affected *us* differently. The stigmata of mutation appeared on my body: it changed and altered. Horns sprouted from my head and my eyes became blind questing stalks. I tore them out and replaced them with magical jewels. But my brain changed too, and my spirit itself was warped. When my hands became talons and my teeth became fangs I was no longer horrified. I gloried in the change and my appetites became . . . abominable. Before, I had been proud and ruthless and, yes, evil; but I had been human. Now, I was a monster.

'Others could not face the changes when they happened. Their minds crumbled, all sanity fled. Many took their own lives, my beloved wife among them. Others became as I and hid themselves from their subjects and customers. It could not last. The common folk rebelled and, though I and my followers put the rebellions down with ever-increasing ferocity, I knew it was only a matter of time before I would be overthrown. So I prepared the Bloodstone, my final folly, a refuge for my spirit against the time of the dissolution of my body.'

Cawlis's heart leapt. Now, at last, he knew Axion's final secret. He had the information needed to make his triumph complete. The part of him that was becoming all too human could not resist speaking out. 'You were overthrown, but we can reclaim your empire. The people still hunger for eternal life. You have already revealed the secret of creating life.'

'Have you heard nothing I have said? There is no secret of eternal life, only the secret of change and mutation and absolute horror.'

'Those things, too, may be good,' Cawlis countered. 'Imagine armies of immortal mutating monsters, able to meet every challenge, changing as their enemy changes, fearing no mortal threat to their dominion.'

'You would not dare!' There was sudden horror and anguish in the manifold voices.

'Would I not, old man? Would I not? You may have grown soft during your centuries of imprisonment in the Bloodstone; I am far stronger!'

'You cannot do this thing! I will not permit it!' The voices babbled, a mixture of fear and anger and sorrow. The intended threat seemed too feeble for Cawlis to show great concern. If he could be sure that he would not need Axion's aid again he would have terminated the mewling creature there and then.

'Be quiet, old man. Your new body is nearly whole. It would be a pity if I had to return you to the Bloodstone now.'

15

Flying High

'I don't like this at all,' Weasel whined, rubbing his swollen and half-closed eye.

'Shut up and help us get this thing into position,' Darkmane said angrily. In part he spoke roughly because he still had not forgiven the little man for spying on Star while she bathed that morning; in part, because he was embarrassed at losing control and giving Weasel a thrashing. He had never behaved this way before. Why did the thought of Weasel lusting after the Elf girl upset him so? Was he simply jealous? Darkmane dismissed the thought immediately and gave all his attention to attaching the heaving gas-bag to the gondola. As he did so, he tested each of the fastening hooks for strength. He did not want them giving way once the balloon was airborne.

'Hey, be careful. Those things took me weeks to make.' Elumbar grinned as he chided the warrior.

Darkmane glared at the Elf. The last light of the sun caught his pink-tinted glasses. The reflection turned his eyes into two tiny, solar orbs. Was this drink-addled nitwit really capable of building a working flying

155

machine, Darkmane wondered. Yaztromo thought so, but the warrior was beginning to have doubts about the old wizard's state of mind. All day long he had been as quiet as the grave, saying little and nodding absent-mindedly whenever Darkmane tried to discuss their strategy for entering the enemy's fortress.

What ailed him? Did the old man have some presentiment of doom? Or had he just drunk too much of Elumbar's potent wine the night before? And why had he come back with his face a picture of glumness after talking with Vermithrax in secret that afternoon? It irked Darkmane that Yaztromo felt it necessary to hold any discussions that he was not party to. Still, he must have his reasons. Perhaps he did not trust Weasel or Elumbar. Darkmane certainly found that easy to understand.

Star busied herself

tightening the guy-wires that linked the strange, bird-like tail of the flying machine to the rest of the craft. Noticing his eyes upon her, she stopped, put her hands on her hips and gave him a look somewhere between a smile and a disappointed grimace. Darkmane wondered if she was still annoyed at him for declining her offer of a moonlight stroll through the forest. He himself wondered at his reluctance to be alone with her. There was something about her hungry eyes and secretive smile that he found deeply unsettling. Not unappealing ... just ... disturbing.

Even Vermithrax was unsettled this evening. The crow kept hopping about on the ground, then taking to the air and circling warily. Strangely enough, he seemed more concerned to keep an eye on the party than to scout out any possible

lurking threats. The atmosphere round Elumbar's home had worked on even Darkmane's iron nerves till he felt nervous and unsettled.

Elumbar finished checking the silk of the gas-bag and wandered off towards the painted trees that lined the edge of the woods. He stood there for a moment, then took off his glasses and peered into the gathering gloom. He polished the spectacles on the hem of his robe before replacing them on the bridge of his nose. He had not touched his wine all day and his attitude could almost be described as business-like, were it not for his constant interrupting of the preparations to wander off and look for his cat.

'Can't understand it,' Elumbar said as he returned, shoulders slumped. 'Cat doesn't usually stay away this long. Hope he hasn't had an accident. Maybe I should go and take a look in the . . .'

'You can do that later,' Darkmane snapped. 'At this moment we have more important things to worry about.'

The Elf shrugged and returned to inspecting his creation. 'I think you should be all right. No flaws that I can see. But then, well, I've thought that before.'

'Oh that's great! That's just fine!' said Weasel, clapping his hands together in sarcastic glee. 'We're about to risk our lives invading the lair of some god-hating sorcerer and *he* has doubts about his flying machine. Typical of an Elf. Completely unreliable. They lead you on with fine promises, but when it comes to the pay-off . . .'

'What are you talking about?' asked Darkmane. He noticed that Star was giving Weasel a funny look. Yaztromo too was looking on interestedly.

'Oh, nothing. But if I'm going to risk my life in this

contraption, I'd like its builder to show a little more faith, if you know what I mean.'

'You don't have to come with us, little man. In fact, I'd be quite glad if you didn't,' Darkmane reminded him.

'Oh no! You can't wriggle out of having to pay me so easily. And I want my share of that sorcerer's treasure too.'

It was obvious that Weasel had convinced himself that the only reason for Darkmane and Yaztromo seeking out Hellsgate Keep was to plunder it. The idea that they might have more noble reasons did not seem to have occurred to him. Did he judge everyone by his own low standards, Darkmane wondered. What a terrible way to live a life.

'He's got to come with us, Chadda,' said Yaztromo. 'It takes four to steer the balloon.'

'We could take Elumbar.'

'Oh no,' said the Elf. 'I wouldn't want to risk flying in . . . I mean, I don't think I would be much use in Hellsgate. Fighting evil sorcerers is not really my scene, you see. I prefer to focus positive ethereal vibrations at them from a distance.'

'Does it work?' Darkmane asked.

'Well, you'll see when you get there.'

'I guessed you might say that.'

'Does *she* have to come? It's unlucky to have women on ships,' Weasel said, pointing at Star. The Elf glared back at him, then moved over to stand in Darkmane's shadow. He was uncomfortably aware of her proximity.

'I suppose you learned that from the ocean nomads of the desert too?' Darkmane enquired sarcastically.

'Yes — I mean, no. Oh, what's the use? Anyone can see you're enamoured of the Elvi—'

'WHAT?' Darkmane's roar surprised even himself. He

felt his cheeks burning red and he was half-way to Weasel before Yaztromo intervened.

'Be calm, Chadda. He meant nothing. 'Twas only a jibe, meant to annoy you. He did not mean anything by it. Did you, Weasel?'

'No. It was only a joke, Chadda, old mate. No need to take it so seriously. Just a joke. I'm famous for my jokes, me.'

Darkmane realized he was making a fool of himself and stopped in his tracks. He controlled his temper with an effort. There was no Amonour to be gained in giving Weasel a beating. He just wished that Star had not been there to hear what the little man had said and see his own reaction to it. Swiftly he turned to face her. 'You don't have to come with us,' he said. 'I'm strong enough to steer for two.'

'I know you are,' she cooed softly. 'But I would not miss going with you for the world.'

'All right; but when we get there, you stay with the balloon. It could be very dangerous.'

'I don't care. As long as I'm with you, I'd go any-where.'

'Best hurry then,' said Elumbar, 'for the sun's nearly down. Here, Cat! Where are you, Cat! I've got some nice fish for your tea!'

Overhead Vermithrax cawed ominously.

'Ready then?' Elumbar said. Darkmane nodded nervously. His hand was still glowing from clasping Star's while helping her over the side of the gondola.

'As I'm ever going to be,' Weasel said nervously.

'Well, get ready. We're going to ignite the herbs now.' Elumbar took the taper and handed it to Yaztromo. The mage applied it to the burner. A pungent aroma of herbs and charcoal filled the air as the brazier took light. The rush of hot air filled the gondola. Darkmane felt his eyes begin to smart as the heat hit his face.

Slowly at first, then more quickly, the balloon started to inflate, rising above them like a huge, fast-growing fungus. As it did so, the basket started to bob up and down like a cork on the surface of a choppy sea. The ropes pinning it to the ground creaked with the strain.

Weasel gave a little shriek.

'Hold on! I'm going to release the pins,' Elumbar shouted. 'Peace and the good gods go with you!'

As the first two ropes were released, the gondola tipped sideways. Darkmane threw out a hand to hold the side of the basket. With the other he caught Star as she was thrown against him.

'Ah-whoaaaa!' Weasel's panicky voice rang out. Star threw her arm round Darkmane's waist as the third pin was released. The balloon was rising fast now and the last rope gave way under its impetus. Darkmane's stomach gave a lurch as they took off. It was the strangest sensation, watching the ground drift away beneath them, seeing Elumbar dwindle until he was a tiny stick-man on the shadowy ground. The Elf waved up at them, but Darkmane resisted the urge to wave back.

'Oh, demon's breath!' wailed Weasel. 'I think I'm going to be sick!'

Vermithrax circled the balloon and Darkmane concentrated on keeping him in view. It somehow helped to have a stable point of reference as they ascended. The basket in which they stood felt so fragile, rocking with every motion of the flying machine. He was uncomfortably aware that there was little more than a carpet of matting and wood between him and a long fall to the ground. Memories of his time on Zharradan Marr's flying *Galleykeep* came flooding back. Even that had not been so bad; that craft had been huge and stable, so large that one never doubted that one was suspended safely, high above the ground. It had felt like an island in the sky. Once you accepted the fact that you were up there, you never questioned that it was going to stay aloft.

Elumbar's craft, on the other hand, was tiny, a mere coracle of the skies, at the mercy of every current of air and wind. The slightest turbulence buffeted the craft, rocking it from side to side, and with every swaying motion Darkmane felt as though his stomach was about to leap into his throat.

Slowly he disentangled himself from Star and moved away from the edge of the basket. He began to feel better . . . until he almost backed into the brazier.

The balloon drifted slowly across the sky. Beneath them, the silver moonlight washed the forest, turning the wood into an enchanted realm of mystery. From below came the sounds of breaking undergrowth and ferocious struggle as an unseen night predator stalked and trapped its prey.

Darkmane leaned against the tiller and pushed with all his strength. The tail-planes creaked and the flying machine adjusted its course a fraction. Ahead of them, far in the distance, were the looming crags of Hellsgate, dark talons reaching threateningly towards the enormous moon. Darkmane shivered a little – from the cold, he reassured himself.

The brazier flickered and burned low. Little blue flames danced over the charcoal. Darkmane noticed Yaztromo peering at him across the fire. His face was lit from below, all the stark angles showing, seemingly carved from solid stone. His eyes glittered, as cold as stars in a polar sky. He looked immeasurably old, both sinister and wise. Darkmane wondered at his own decision to trust this aged sorcerer; at his ability to put aside his normal reservations and co-operate with the old man's plans. Once he would have laughed if anyone had told him that one day he would call a mage his friend. *We all change*, he thought. *It's the way life is.*

He looked down at Star. The woman was crouched in the bottom of the basket, staring at him fixedly, as if she had never seen his like before and wanted to etch every detail into her memory. Weasel was huddled against her, head on her shoulder, clutching her like a child clinging to its mother for warmth and reassurance. Occasionally his hands would wander, and Star would firmly remove them; but the gondola was cramped and there was no room for her to move far away from his clutches.

Yaztromo reached out across the brazier, his hand open, palm down, as if testing how hot the flame was. Then he nodded to himself and muttered an incantation. Hissing, the flames spurted upwards, enveloping his hand, leaping so high that Darkmane feared they would engulf the silken gas-bag above. Startled by the flames' sudden roar, Weasel shrieked and scuttled into a corner. The basket swayed and Darkmane struggled to keep his balance.

'What are you doing, Gereth?' he demanded of the sorcerer, old suspicions of magic and mages flooding back. 'Are you trying to kill us all?'

'No, Chadda,' said Yaztromo, rising. Fire blazed from his hand, somehow transferred from the brazier to his clenched fist, although his hand did not scorch and shrivel. Standing there, clutching fire as if it were a dagger, he looked profoundly unnatural. 'The brazier was burning low. We were losing height. If we are to reach the crags, we must maintain our altitude, otherwise we will be dashed on the cliff-face.'

'We are high enough,' said Darkmane. 'We do not need any sorcerous assistance. We would have made it. You almost set the bag alight.'

His words sounded hollow, even to himself.

'I agree with Darkmane,' Weasel said sneakily.

'Then you are both wrong. I know whereof I speak. You will just have to trust me.'

'It seems we have little choice,' said Star. Silence fell over them like a shroud. The balloon drifted on.

16

Into the Hellsgate

Silent as a great shadow, the balloon drifted closer to the dark towers of Hellsgate Keep. Darkmane kept his eyes peeled for sentries, but no sign of life was visible on the forbidding battlements. The towers were as quiet as a cemetery. It was as though all life had departed them centuries back, never to return.

'So far, so good,' he whispered, well aware that the others did not share his confidence. As they approached, Weasel had started muttering prayers to whatever gods might be listening, and Star had clutched his hand desperately. Only Yaztromo seemed to share his quiet resolution, and who really knew what the wizard was thinking?

'Aim for the top of that tower. I can see a flat expanse there,' murmured the wizard. 'You two, help Darkmane.'

They bent their weight to the tiller, and the balloon came around, riding the air-currents smoothly. As the tower approached, the flames on Yaztromo's hands dimmed and the flying machine slowly lost height.

Darkmane thought they were going to overshoot the tower, it loomed so swiftly out of the murk. He heard

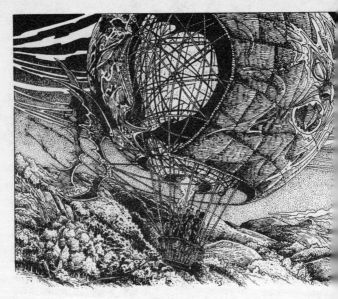

Yaztromo curse and the flame went out entirely. They skimmed down at an alarming speed. Darkmane had to force himself not to shut his eyes. They made contact sharply and the gondola scraped across the stone, yawing alarmingly. Darkmane leapt clear.

No longer held down by his weight, the balloon lurched skywards again. The warrior leapt up and caught one of the trailing ropes. His muscles swelling with the exertion, he wrestled with the rising craft. It felt as if he was trying to restrain a wild bull. Sweat blinded him; agony and fatigue seared his biceps.

'Hold on, Chadda. Hold on!' Star urged. She leapt lithely from the basket and landed beside him. The pressure on his muscles relaxed as she added her weight to his. The gas-bag continued to deflate, as if punctured. Slowly it toppled and fell like a great tree crashing down in slow motion. Then and only then did Weasel get out.

'Thought we weren't going to make it there for a moment, you know what I mean? By all the gods, it surely is good to feel solid earth beneath my feet again, even if it is in this accursed spot!'

Darkmane was forced to agree with him. After hours in the airship he felt a little giddy. His legs had become accustomed to bracing him against the slightest roll of their craft, and now he felt unsteady, anticipating at any moment some lurch of the stone beneath his feet.

Yaztromo emerged from the gondola. He looked pale and a little drained. The strain of keeping the balloon aloft for such a long time had started to show. His eyes glittered feverishly and his cheeks were sunken and hollow.

'There must be a way down near here somewhere. You, Star, stay here.'

'I'll stay here with her,' said Weasel eagerly. 'I'll help her watch the balloon.'

'You're coming with us,' Darkmane said brusquely. 'Perhaps you'll find some treasure.'

'Can't spend treasure when you're dead, mate.'

Vermithrax alighted on the battlements, glanced at Star warily, then preened his feathers. 'C-rawk! Stairs! Near by! Come on!'

Darkmane pointed at the balloon. 'Remember, Star, wait here till we return!'

'And make sure it's us,' added Weasel. Following Vermithrax, they made their way to the stairwell and down into the darkness.

Cawlis gazed upon the pods and smiled. The Shapechanger reached out and felt the moist surface of one with a pale, slender hand. Within the dark and slimy skin something kicked, nearly ready to be born. The umbilical tubes were huge now, swollen with nutrients and covered in a tiny web of purple veins. Adding the sap from the deep wells had made all the difference. The things fairly pulsed with life. *So soon*, he thought, *so soon*.

He followed the great ridged pipes from the nursery chambers to the nutrient vats. For a long moment he stood watching as the Goblins threw new bodies into the cauldrons. They fizzed as powerful alchemical elements reduced them swiftly to a protoplasmic stew.

'Master,' said the Troll commander, who had been supervising the disposal of the new arrivals.

'Excellent work,' said Cawlis jubilantly. 'You've done so very well.'

The Troll almost glowed at this unexpected praise. He inspected his master as closely as he dared, wondering at the Shapechanger's exultant manner.

'We have another raiding party ready to go. I will lead this one myself. If you wish it.'

Into the Hellsgate

'Good! Good! Yes, you may go. I know how you do enjoy your little forays into the outside world.'

'Things go well down below, then?' Seeing his master was so well disposed, he risked a question.

'Beyond all doubt. Better than I could have expected. Now that Axion has revealed his last secret, he can safely be forgotten. His time is done; I can be rid of him. Soon my new servants will be born, and a new order will arise to claim the world. We will lay waste to this ridiculous, petty mudball and begin an age-long night of terror such as the world has never seen.'

The Troll averted his eyes; his master's face seemed to shine with an inner light. There was a power about him that the Troll had never sensed before, something that made his mad, exultant words seem not only believable but inevitable.

'I shall go and inform the men of your instructions, lord.'

The Troll hurried away. The echoes of his footsteps were drowned out by the sound of his master's triumphant laughter.

Weasel looked to the left. Weasel darted a glance to the right. Weasel looked behind him — and started at the sight of his own shadow. The flickering light from the strange torches inset in the wall made the shadow caper grotesquely. He turned and hurried down the corridor after Darkmane.

How did I ever get myself involved in this? he wondered. *Me, poor, pitiful Weasel who never harmed a soul in his life. In a life full of unfairness and dogged with unjust punishments, this is all but unbearable. I didn't ask to come here. No. I warned them about it, but they had to come seeking treasure. No good will come of it, I said, but would they listen? Oh no, they knew better.*

Shadowmaster

I should be up there on the surface, protecting poor Star, helping to keep her warm, not down here in these dark, musty depths, jumping at shadows and the slightest sound.

Not that I'm scared. The bold Weasel goes where others fear to tread. Nothing frightens him. What was that? No, no need to worry. It was nothing, only the rock settling.

By the gods, I hope it doesn't collapse. Who can tell? It might. Everyone knows Dwarfish workmanship can be very shoddy. I don't care what that old Yazz says. It's stood for centuries, indeed. What does that mumbling old fake know, eh? If it's stood for centuries, that just means it's very old, doesn't it? Stands to reason. And if it's old, it could collapse at any time, just like that old pile of ruins I sold Johan Vander, heh-heh! What an idiot he was. He was so stupid he was practically begging me to part him from his money. Well, someone else would have taken it if I hadn't, so it was only fair really. Better a deserving Weasel than some undeserving confidence trickster. And the money was well spent — what a time young Justina and I had, eh? Now there was a tricksy piece of baggage. Not as pretty as that Elf upstairs, true, but a lovely wench all the same. And I liked her, even if she did make off with my purse while I was asleep. Not that she fooled me for a second, of course — it was just my way of giving her a pleasant farewell.

Yes, but isn't that Star a looker, though? No wonder even that stuck-up prig Darkmane is sweet on her. Even seen old Yazz give her a funny look now and again. No goat worse than an old goat, that's what I always say.

Hang on! Where did they go? There's the light up ahead. Hang on, wait for me! What was that, down that side-passage? Probably nothing. After all, what could sneak up on the ever-alert Weasel, eh?

Thra-zat watched the small stranger disappear after his

companions. For a second he had feared he had been spotted. That would have been bad, for there were no big ones about to protect Thra-zat.

He flexed his ears, and slowly it dawned on him. Strangers! Thra-zat wondered whether he should inform one of the big ones. Perhaps this was important, so important that this time they wouldn't pull his pretty ears or tear off some of his arm scales. Strangers shouldn't be here, not live ones anyway. The only strangers allowed were dead ones, to be thrown into the pots that fed the scary ones. Thra-zat didn't like the scary ones. Maybe they wouldn't be pleased if they found out their food was walking about upstairs. No, definitely he should tell someone.

Who to tell? He wracked his brain for someone to tell this important piece of news to, preferably someone who wouldn't pull his ears or steal his scales. Should he tell the big boss? If it was really important, he would be rewarded. The thought of a reward made his ears swell up. It might be a big reward — maybe even, if he was especially lucky, a double ration of rat for his supper. That would be good. He could take it away and hide from the big ones and maybe even get to eat it. Yes, definitely, he must take his news to the big boss.

So thinking, Thra-zat scuttled off down the corridor, the vision of two rats floating deliciously through his tiny brain.

Darkmane stared warily into the chamber. His suspicious had proved to be correct: there were guards here. Four bloated Orcs lounged around, leaning on their notched scimitars. Slovenly creatures, thought Darkmane, wondering who would trust such lazy animals for guard duty.

He glanced back and signalled for Yaztromo and

Weasel to ready themselves. One swift charge across the room, a flurry of blows, and they could pass on. It all seemed perfectly straightforward. The odds were four to three. With the element of surprise on their side, he did not doubt that he could handle three of them, and Weasel and the wizard should be able to take care of the fourth.

A clattering noise from behind alerted him that all was not well. He turned to see Weasel and the wizard entangled together. The little man was puffing and out of breath; he had obviously just come running up and had banged into the wizard and Yaztromo had dropped his staff. Worse still, the noise had alerted the Orcs. Darkmane cursed silently. His luck seemed to be running true to form for this expedition. It was funny, though, how bad luck always seemed to involve

Weasel. If the Orcs didn't take care of the broken-toothed little idiot, perhaps he would do so himself.

Then he had no time for more thoughts: the Orcs were upon him. He blocked the swing of one scimitar and stepped aside, letting the blow from the next whistle harmlessly by him. Then he knocked the first Orc's weapon aside and stabbed him through the heart. Gurgling, the creature fell. Darkmane struggled to pull his blade from its recumbent form as the other two rushed forward.

From behind him he heard Weasel's frantic shriek as he was forced to engage the Orc Darkmane had side-stepped. With a sickening sucking sound, his blade came free. He swung it two-handed at his oncoming foes. One attempted a parry and had his blade battered aside, while the

other snarled and came on, stepping smartly inside the arc of Darkmane's blade.

Chadda's next blow severed the arm of its partner, and he wheeled to face his third opponent. Behind, he could see Weasel engaged in a desperate struggle while Yaztromo, white-faced and perspiring, futilely mouthed the words of a spell. A faint glow surrounded the old man's hand but, like a guttering candle in a draughty house, it flickered and vanished.

His last foe was tougher than the first two, more experienced and therefore wary. It feinted a high blow then, at the last second, brought its scimitar sweeping in low. Darkmane was the veteran of too many conflicts to fall for that ploy. He stepped back out of range, then, giving vent to all the anger and tension he had felt from the moment he first entered these dank caverns, he unleashed an irresistible attack.

The Orc might as well have tried to parry chain lightning. Darkmane's attack was sight-blurringly swift and propelled by an arm as strong as a Troll's. The creature tried an ineffectual parry, then fell to its knees clutching the stump where its hand had been. Darkmane finished it off with his return stroke. As he did so, he saw the last Orc fall. Weasel's somewhat unorthodox strategy had been to throw himself flat on the ground as if about to plead for mercy; then, by what appeared to be complete accident, his flailing blade had caught the creature's ankle, hamstringing it. Once it had fallen, Weasel rose to his feet, a look of complete shock on his face, and finished it off.

'Fat lot of use you were,' he said, turning on Yaztromo with all the venom that fear makes possible. 'Standing there mumbling. That thing could have killed me, you know what I mean?'

Into the Hellsgate

Darkmane peered at the old wizard with concern. Yaztromo looked even more pale and shrivelled than he had at the top of the tower. It was as if all the strength had drained out of him. When he spoke, his voice was a weak croak.

'Chadda, there is some force present here, as there was back in Drystone. My magic is being suppressed!'

Cawlis stood with his eyes shut and listened to the words of the Goblin-thing, Thra-zat. His sergeants must have thought the little creature's message important or they would not have allowed it to disturb him. He hoped it *was* important, for their sakes.

'Yes, yes, master. Thra-zat saw them. Three strangers. Big man, dark hair, many muscles. Old man, beard and staff. Bird was with old man. Big black crow bird. Weak man, little and lost, hurrying down long passageway. Thra-zat is not lying. Not make up story just to get extra rat. Thra-zat saw with own eyes. True.'

An old man with a crow for a familiar, thought Cawlis, accompanied by a muscular warrior. It could only be the two he had fought in Drystone. That explained the familiar sense of a magical presence that had been nagging at the corners of his mind for the past few hours.

'Thank you, little one. You have confirmed my suspicions. I felt him, just as I sensed his presence at Drystone. Now they will be dealt with. You may go.'

'Reward, master! Extra rat! Extra rat!'

'Certainly, little one! You have done well this day. Have two.' Cawlis was feeling generous. Things were going his way. Not only did he have Axion's secrets, but soon he would have revenge on that arrogant warrior who had escaped him at Drystone.

*

'Back,' Darkmane snapped, allowing a trace of urgency to reveal itself in his voice. It was too late; the large party of raiders had seen them. Even as he spoke, their Troll leader bellowed an order. Screaming war-cries, the bandits charged across the great underground hall. Darkmane had a brief impression of a vast chamber with an arched ceiling, its walls surrounded by tapestries. It provided a backdrop for a collection of surprised faces out of the worst nightmares of a madman: twisted Orc visages with tusks jutting from their lower lips and great wattles depending from their jaws; sly Goblin features with reddish eyes glittering in deep sockets; scaly Lizard Men with jaws like lanterns and teeth like a shark's.

There were too many monsters in that company for even Chadda Darkmane to contemplate fighting. He turned on his heel and prepared to order the others to run, but Weasel had already bolted down the corridor, and Yaztromo was following him. Vermithrax was a dark shadow receding into the even darker shadows in the middle distance.

It was obvious that the old man was already tired. As he accelerated past him, Darkmane swept him up under one arm and bore him along. The wizard was not a light man; years of good living had added considerably to his girth, yet Darkmane carried him as easily as if he were a child, his stride not faltering as he raced along through the mountain's black heart.

Behind him the bandits yelled triumphantly, howls torn from their throats by the excitement of the chase. Darkmane was reminded of a pack of hounds chasing a fox during a hunt he had once witnessed. As he ran, he was uncomfortably reminded how that particular pursuit had ended, with the maddened dogs tearing their pitiful victim limb from limb. Well, he thought grimly, if his pursuers caught up with him, they would find they had caught a wolf, not a fox. Still, best not to get caught at all.

Burdened as he was, Darkmane swiftly overtook Weasel. 'Right!' he shouted as they came to a junction. Weasel dithered for a moment, then leapt in the direction indicated. Darkmane was glad; he could not let even so despicable a creature as Weasel fall into the hands of their foul pursuers.

'This isn't very dignified for a mage of my years and reputation,' Yaztromo gasped. His weight was starting to be a burden on even Darkmane's iron strength.

'I could always put you down,' he said, and cursed himself for wasting breath he needed for running. His chest was beginning to burn like a blacksmith's forge from the effort. Sweat ran down the curve of his spine. His legs ached from the shock of their impact on the hard stone.

'That will not be necessary. Oh, if only I could muster a spell, but my head aches and the power will not flow.'

They passed many barred doors. As Darkmane ran he beat on them with his fists, but they would not open. All he got for his effort was a sore hand. 'Locked,' he cursed. No place to hide.

'Wait for me,' wailed Weasel. The sound of pursuit was receding a little. The bandits could not match Darkmane's long stride, and terror had given Weasel's feet wings. Only Vermithrax seemed to be enjoying himself.

'Crawwwrk! This is fun! Wheee! Silly Orclings will never catch meeee! Craaark!'

'I'll ring your neck, you semi-evolved lizard,' muttered the old sorcerer.

You might have to beat me to it, thought Darkmane.

The crow banked to the right at the next bend, gliding round the corner in a long, smooth curve. Darkmane's boots skidded around after him. He put out his sword hand to stop himself from slamming into the wall. Yaztromo's weight was proving too much, and Darkmane let him down as gently as possible. The yelps and yowls of their pursuers came ever closer.

'Run!' Darkmane ordered. Wheezing and puffing, the old man followed. Darkmane forced himself to jog at the wizard's pace. It was no use; their foes would soon overtake them. It was going to take a miracle to save them now.

They came to another junction. From the left came the sound of hurrying, scurrying feet. The alarm had obviously been sounded now, and reinforcements were on their way, not that they were needed. Darkmane was not afraid to die; his only regret was that he would not get a chance to look on Star's face again. Now why did that thought occur to him now of all times?

'Leave me . . .' Yaztromo wheezed, stretching out his hand in entreaty. As he did so, Weasel squeezed past and sprinted away down the corridor. 'Save yourself. Without my magic I am no use to you anyway.'

'Chadda Darkmane never abandoned a friend,' his companion muttered. He scooped up the wizard and ran to the right. The hounds were overtaking him, he realized. The wizard's weight was slowing him down too much. On his own he could escape, perhaps. Firmly he pushed the thought aside; there was no Amonour to be gained by such a dishonourable deed.

He carried the old man into an enormous, echoing hall. To his horror he realized that it was the very one they had vacated at the start of the chase! Where was Weasel? The little man was not so fleet of foot that he could have crossed the hall and vanished before Dark-mane even arrived. The thunder of their pursuers' foot-steps was growing louder. *Quickly, think of something!* Darkmane told himself. Then he spotted that one of the tapestries was fluttering. Of course! He rushed over and drew the drape aside.

'No! This is my hiding-place!' Weasel shrieked. 'Find your own!'

'No time,' Darkmane replied, pushing Yaztromo into the alcove with them. It was warm and dark here and contained many nooks and crannies. Darkmane hastily pulled the drape back into position just as their pursuers entered the hall.

For a moment the footsteps came to a halt. Darkmane held his breath, trusting the others to keep silent. He heard the Troll rasp out some orders and he opened the hanging a crack. Peering through the slit, he saw the Orcs begin to race off through one of the exits while the Goblins and Lizard Men took the other. The Troll stood in the middle of the chamber, scratching his head in a bemused fashion. Darkmane felt a surge of relief flood through him. If only the others would keep quiet, in a few moments more they would be safe . . .

Two whole rats! Thra-zat gloated. In his whole life he had never dreamed of such luxury. Two whole rats and they were all his, to do with as he liked. What a generous master Lord Cawlis was! Who could have dreamed his information was so valuable? Heh-heh! The stupid big ones would never find him here in his special hiding-place. He wondered where they had gone. Usually a whole gang of them could be found lurking in the hall, waiting for orders from that stupid Troll. He had heard them screaming in the distance, probably off playing

Hunt the Goblin again. Well, he wouldn't question his luck. He would devour his treasures in peace. Two whole rats!

When the drapes parted, he wanted to shriek with rage: the big ones had found him! They would pull his ears and pick off his scales and take his rats. Then he saw it was not a big one. It was the littlest stranger. Thra-zat sank back into the deepest, darkest part of his hideout. The little man didn't seem to have noticed him. Good! Thra-zat would not have to share his food.

Then yet more footsteps came closer. Big ones, Thra-zat thought in fear. They had found him. It was all the little stranger's fault. He had led them right to Thra-zat's rats. Thra-zat was so angry he could have bit the little stranger. Maybe he would taste good ... probably not as nice as rat though.

The drapes parted again. The two big strangers squeezed in, forcing the little stranger back. He was so close that he was virtually on top of Thra-zat. The drapes closed again. Four people in the hideout. Two rats. The arithmetic was not good. Between the four of them, that would mean only one rat apiece. Hold on, that was wrong!

Thra-zat trembled when he heard the Troll's voice. That meant there were definitely big ones present. If Thra-zat could have backed away any further he would have done, but he was already hard up against the cold wall.

The little stranger could. He backed right into Thra-zat, crushing him against the wall with his nasty behind. The big ones began to depart, but still the little stranger did not move. Thra-zat was having trouble breathing. Only one thing for it. He bit the little stranger, sharp teeth sinking into the fleshy rump.

Into the Hellsgate

Weasel gave a shriek of combined agony and terror. The sound of the footsteps ceased, then they came closer. The drapes were pulled aside and the Troll glared down at them.

Oh no, thought Thra-zat, *he's found me, the big bully! He'll take away my rats for sure.*

17

The Bloodstone

Yaztromo looked up into the face of death. The Troll's face was split with a wide grin. Behind him, serried ranks of bandits had drawn up.

Darkmane growled and prepared to launch himself forward to certain death. In the background Weasel was shrieking. 'I'm poisoned! I'm dying! It bit me! It bit me!'

Desperation gave the old wizard strength. He reached down into the very core of his being and sought the secret well of his power. Despite the imposed spell that was trying to inhibit him, he began to draw on it. He raised his hands. A nimbus of light played round his fingers. They felt like lead but he forced them to go through the complex series of ritual gestures. Everything was happening in slow motion.

Darkmane's blade moved in a slow, solemn arc; it had the power and inevitable motion of an asteroid colliding with a planet. The Troll's gaping mouth opened a fraction wider. The enemy troops began to bound forward, jaws open, blades held high. Yaztromo fought to force the spell out. It seemed stuck in his throat, covered in spikes that caught at his weakness. He felt nauseous, as if he was choking, and his heart hammered against his ribs. By force of will he made his lips move. The energy built up within him threatened to make his chest explode. The thought flickered through his mind that the power at work here must be awesome if it could suppress his own magic like this. He pushed the distracting thought to one side, cleared his mind and tried to speak. His vocal cords felt as if they had become rusted in place.

Darkmane's blade had nearly made contact. Too late, the Troll began to back away. The howling horde shuddered ever closer.

Syllable by ponderous syllable, Yaztromo spoke the words. No spell had ever been so difficult to cast since his days as an apprentice to old Vermithrax Moonchaser, his long-dead master. With awful slowness the magic spilled forth. He felt as though he was vomiting. His hand caught fire, blazing more brightly than the sun. The shadows danced away before that dazzling, blinding explosion of light. The monsters shrieked and covered their eyes. The flash passed, leaving the hall dimmed now it was gone.

Yaztromo saw that Darkmane's blade had inflicted a terrible wound on the Troll. 'Come! Let's away,' the sorcerer panted. 'The effect of the flash will not last long.'

Suddenly everything was happening in normal time again. The three companions fled out of the chamber. The dark shadow of the crow, Vermithrax, darted down from his high, hidden ledge and joined them. Behind them they heard the screams of the terrified Orcs, none daring to pursue them.

Cawlis felt the awesome surge of power explode in the depths of his arcane mind. He sat back on his throne and clutched the arm-rests, waiting for the momentary agony to pass. He clenched his teeth and took three deep breaths. Slowly the small silver stars filling his field of vision faded.

Who would have thought the old man capable of it, he thought, at once both amused and a little frightened. There was strength in him yet. *I would not have believed anyone who was not attuned to it capable of overcoming the power of the Bloodstone in this place.* He knew the entire fortress was permeated with its influence. He had drawn on its reserves secretly and subtly to power the defensive spells and shield this place from the divinations of prying wizards.

Ah, Axion, in your day you were truly a titan among mortal mages; to have created the Bloodstone, that source of tremendous mystical potency, and to have penetrated the mysteries of life. One such discovery would have been enough for most mages; you had to make two. And still you have tenuous connections with your greatest creation. Were it not for the binding of the nutrient web, even now you might be able to re-assert your control over it. Then you might be even more of a threat than panting old Yaztromo!

He had returned Axion to the room whence he had summoned him; now the nutrients were being drawn out of him again, even while the spell was being reversed. It was a slow process, but Cawlis considered it far better to be safe than sorry.

Soon you will die the true death, Cawlis promised. *Destroyed as you were summoned, strength leeched by the tubes that once fed you. Then I will tear the Bloodstone from your chest and it will be mine to direct as I will.*

The thought made him shiver with pleasure. With an army of unstoppable mutants and the power of the Bloodstone to aid him, nothing could stand in his way.

*

The Bloodstone

'Admit it, we're lost, aren't we?' said Weasel. 'We're lost in this gods-forsaken place. And what are these horrible things, anyway?'

Darkmane glanced at the pulsing chrysalises which lined the walls, then inspected the throbbing pipes of living flesh that fed them. The air here was hot and moist, and the floor itself felt spongy. There was an aura of unspeakable evil about this place. Yaztromo staggered and almost fell. Darkmane held out an arm to support him.

'They're eggs,' the old wizard muttered. 'Hamaskis aid me, what madness is this? What terrible thing is hatching here?'

They stumbled on down the fetid corridor to its end. Before them, a slow pulsing of reddish light could be seen. As they approached, it turned their faces the colour of blood. The hairs on the back of Darkmane's neck crackled upright and there was a tension in the pit of his stomach such as he usually felt only before some major battle. The sour taste of bile filled his mouth.

'I won't go any further,' Weasel announced.

Darkmane did not blame him; there was a sense of palpable evil in the air and a stink that reminded them of decomposing flesh mixed with another, far viler odour. From ahead came a faint murmuring, as of many voices talking to one another. All sounded as if they were in great pain.

'We are nearing the heart of this darkness,' Yaztromo said weakly, 'I can sense it. Be on guard, my friends. We approach something old and terribly cunning in the ways of evil.'

Darkmane forced himself to move. It was as if he were pushing against a tangible barrier, as if something was trying to force him back with every step. His face tingled and his eyes started to water. The stink of corruption became almost overpowering and the air felt as thick as liquid when he forced it into his lungs. He heard Yaztromo's squelching footsteps behind him and Weasel's whimpering. One step at a time, he forced himself to go on.

Darkmane stepped into the chamber and his eyes widened. His jaw went slack and he wanted to scream.

The Troll stood before Cawlis, clutching its wounded side.

'They eluded us, master. The old one cast a spell so potent it overcame all my troops. There was nothing we could do. Our tracking Goblins followed them to the edge of the nursery level. We did not follow. You ordered us not to enter there with the time of hatching so close.'

Cawlis smiled coldly at the Troll. 'Fear not. They will never leave that place alive. Muster your men and find them before they reach the Chamber of Summoning. If they get there, that could spell disaster for us all. Send everyone you can to that level. They must not escape this time.'

'Your will be done, master.'

As the Troll turned to leave, one of his Lizard Man sergeants entered, the spines of his back bristling with urgency.

'Master, master! Our patrols on the battlements have found another intruder.'

'Excellent,' said Cawlis in his softest and politest voice. 'You are to be commended.'

'It is most strange, master. She claims to be one of us.'

'Does she, indeed? Well, well. Bring her to me!'

*

The Bloodstone

'Is it dead?' Weasel asked, staring up at the huge, horned shape. The voices had stopped when Darkmane entered the chamber. Sick with horror, he stared, wide-eyed at the massive, taloned form which lay on the slab in the middle of a web of veins, each as thick as a wriggling worm. Within its chest something was pulsing hypnotically; it was the source of the dim red light that illuminated the horrible chamber.

'I have seen some dreadful things in my time,' said Yaztromo, 'but none of them . . ' His voice trailed off. There were no words to describe his horror.

'This is against all the laws of life,' said Darkmane. Something about the light source drew his eye. Somehow he could make out the form of a great egg-shaped gem within the creature's chest. Somewhere in the back of his mind he began to feel a compulsion to reach out, to touch it.

'I sense dark magic about this,' said Weasel.

'Very observant, O best of guides,' Darkmane said absent-mindedly, reaching out for the gem. His hand had almost reached the creature's chest when Yaztromo grabbed his wrist.

'No, Chadda! Its magic is too strong even for me. It must not touch your naked flesh. I can sense the power of the sorcery behind it!'

At the mention of the word 'sorcery' Darkmane emerged from his trance with an involuntary gasp. He had always mistrusted the dark power of magic. What was he thinking about to be trying to snatch the gem?

Yaztromo reached out and took Weasel's scarf from him. He began to wrap it round Darkmane's hand. Weasel noticed what was happening and whirled around.

'Oi! That's my best scarf. Give it back, you wicked old thief.'

Yaztromo's voice was low and dangerous now, his eyes the grey-blue of tempered steel. 'Some day I will tell you what happened to the last man who called me a thief. Suffice to say for the moment, little man, that it was not pleasant.'

'Sorry. It's my nerves. They're a little on edge, you know what I mean? It's this place. No offence. Take the scarf if you can use it. Here, have my belt too. I don't need it, honest.'

'That will not be necessary,' Yaztromo replied coldly.

With his hand bound by Weasel's filthy scarf, Dark-mane reached out once more for the Bloodstone. The flesh of the creature's chest cavity was brittle and cracked easily. Slowly, gently, as if wishing not to disturb a sleeper, he reached out and took the gem. Even through the cloth its power made his fingers tingle. He lifted it up in the air. Seeing a gem as big as an egg in Darkmane's hand, Weasel gasped aloud.

A taloned hand reached up and made a grab for Darkmane's wrist.

Just in the nick of time the warrior snatched his hand back as the disgusting figure on the table began to rise. Darkmane backed away in horror and surprise. Five voices babbled at once: 'No heart give my heart no! Give me back my heart!'

Weasel leapt forward, showing surprising presence of mind – or perhaps it was only the confusion of panic. He pushed the creature off the slab so that it dangled in the air, suspended by the web of veins, veins which slowly began to stretch and part. A crackle of ferocious magical energy filled the air.

'Quick, break those pipes, they are all that is keeping it alive,' Yaztromo shouted. Darkmane's blade flicked out, severing the veins. Dark liquid sprayed everywhere, filling the room with a fine drizzle of vile-smelling fluid.

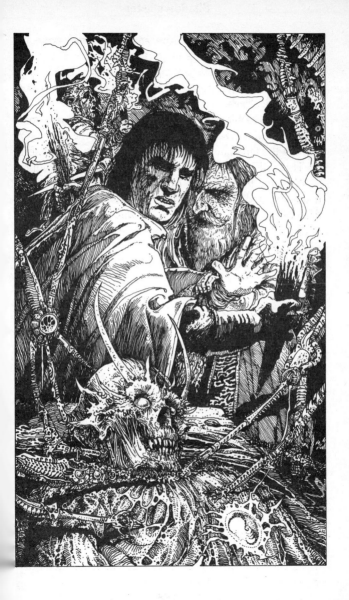

The voices roared out, 'Wrong, mage! They were the only things binding me!'

The horrific, deathless figure of Axion surged to its feet, an image of pure terror towering a head above Darkmane. Fleshless jaws grinned in a skeletal face. Jewelled eyes blazed with malevolent life. As one man, the heroes turned and fled.

18

Things That Crawl

Fleeing headlong from the chamber of the creature, they raced through the darkened corridors. All around, the pods bubbled and writhed.

'I don't like this at all,' Weasel moaned as they ran.

'They're going to hatch. We'd best get out of here,' Yaztromo advised him.

'I'm with you, Yazz,' agreed Weasel.

Yaztromo was exhausted now, more tired than he had ever been. Was he dying, he wondered, or was it simply the baleful influence of their surroundings? Darkmane seemed distracted, his face contorted by an internal fury; the hellish light from the Bloodstone made his face look almost demonic. Yaztromo knew that his friend resented having to flee from the unholy animated corpse of the long-dead sorcerer. Giving way to a moment of stark terror was not something that was supposed to happen to a true warrior of Salamonis; it was bad for his Amonour. Well, young Chadda was learning. No one is perfect. No one should be without fear when fear is the only sensible emotion to have.

Yaztromo needed time to rest; strength seeped from

him like wine from an overturned goblet. He felt dizzy and his mind was growing fuzzy. 'Which way did we come?' he asked, his mind reeling, his vision fading in and out of focus. *Get a hold of yourself, old man. You still have work to do.*

'This way,' said Weasel, pointing to the left.

'No, this way,' Darkmane countered, immediately setting off to the right. The wizard lurched after him.

'Well, don't say I didn't warn you,' the little man said, scuttling after them. Even through the cloth of Weasel's scarf, Yaztromo could see the glow of the Bloodstone, brighter now than it had been before. Why did it grow brighter as he grew weaker, Yaztromo wondered.

He could sense the power of the thing, its sheer malevolence, gnawing at the edges of his mind. He was glad Darkmane was carrying it; he would be afraid to touch such a thing. It seemed to have a life of its own, as if it had been impregnated with the personality of its long-time inhabitant. And why not, he thought. People leave traces of their auras where they have lived for a long time, all diviners knew that. The Bloodstone had contained part of the spirit of Axion for centuries; it was bound to hold some psychic echo of his inhuman evil.

There were fewer pods around now, and those there were seemed smaller. Apparently they had reached the outer limits of the experimental chambers. Yaztromo thanked all the gods for that. Now, all they had to do was climb these stairs and with luck they would get away before the things hatched. He only hoped he had the strength to mount them. He could not ask Darkmane to carry him again; the warrior needed one hand to hold the Bloodstone and the other to fight. The wizard was not sure why he felt the gem was the key to their whole predicament, but he was wise enough to put his trust in such a strong intuition . . . at least, he hoped that's what it was. What if the Bloodstone was playing tricks on his mind?

'Vermithrax, scout ahead,' the old man croaked. 'Make sure nothing awaits us at the head of the stairs!'

'Yes, Yaaaz! C-rawk!' The crow soared upwards into the gloom. The three men rested for a moment at the foot of the steps.

'Think we've got away from old bonehead then?' Weasel asked, staring nervously back down the corridors. It was clear he did not know which to fear more: the resurrected mage or the pods that were threatening to hatch.

'I hope we find him,' Darkmane spat out the words angrily. 'This time I'm ready for him.'

'He's all yours, friend,' Weasel scowled.

'How are you, Gereth? Is your magic power still beyond you? Loath as I am to say it, I fear we may need to call upon it before the end.'

There's hope for you yet, Chadda Darkmane, thought the wizard. Under other circumstances he could almost have smiled. It was not like the grim warrior to admit that he might be mistaken.

'I may be able to manage a spell or two. I do feel a little better,' Yaztromo lied. He felt that if he made any attempt to use his own powers, it would kill him, leave him torn apart and unable to control his own magic. If only he could find a way to tap the energy of the Bloodstone. If only. Perhaps . . .

Vermithrax returned.

'C-rawk. Not this way! Many monsters! Many, many monsters!'

Darkmane jumped to his feet and stared balefully up the stairs. His blade was held firmly in his mighty grasp.

'This time we fight!' he said, determination blazing in his voice.

'This time we run!' Weasel shouted, grasping Yaztromo's hand and dragging him back down the corridor. Darkmane paused for only a moment before joining them.

'You have no Amonour, little man!' he called out contemptuously, but he followed them just the same. As they re-entered the hatching chambers, Yaztromo noticed that one of the chrysalises had split. Yellow liquid had leaked from a crack in its slimy, leathery carapace and was dribbling on to the spongy ground.

Cawlis strode towards the entrance of the nursery levels, anger etched into every angle of his narrow face. Things were starting to go terribly wrong. He could no longer sense Axion's presence. Had the Master of Shadows expired or was something else taking place about which he had no knowledge? Part of Cawlis was more than human enough now to be worried.

'Master, they have fled down into the underlevel once more,' his Troll commander reported nervously. He lurched along behind Cawlis at the head of his personal bodyguard. *There was something pitiful about so large a creature trying to fawn*, Cawlis thought. *Perhaps once this was over he should put it out of its misery. Yes, that would probably be best.*

'Let us hurry, then,' he said calmly. 'We have a surprise to prepare for them. If you succeed now, I will forgive you your past failures. If you fail . . .'

The Troll looked away. Cawlis could guess what it was thinking. Despite it all, he smiled.

Vermithrax came flapping back down the corridor like a feathered thunderbolt.

Things That Crawl

'C-rawk! I've found another way to the surface, Yaaaz! I found another way up!'

Yaztromo felt a surge of relief. He didn't like these chambers, full of chrysalises, any more than Weasel did, and he was sure his raddled senses were telling him that the power which had been present in Drystone was approaching once again. If they could reach the balloon and escape this well-named hellish place, he would have time to rest and plan, and find a way to overcome their opponents.

'Ulp! This isn't looking good, fellows,' Weasel said queasily. The pods along the walls were cracking open. As he hurried past, Yaztromo thought he saw an ivory claw, whiter than bone, gleaming through the slit in one straining pod.

'How much further, my faithful pet?' he asked.

'C-rawk! Two more chambers, master.'

'Then let us make haste.'

In the final chamber they paused, too horrified to continue. The pods were bursting open before their terror-widened eyes. Each made a noise like cloth tearing, and the air was full of a nauseating, sickly-sweet smell. Slowly the hatchlings were peeling back flaps in the chrysalises. They pulled themselves out of the eggs, dripping a substance that reminded the mage of the white of an egg. Hideous beaked mouths gaped to draw in their first breaths. Talons flexed, enjoying new-found freedom. Like baby lizards hatching into the sun they came. They were scaled and clawed and horned.

There were dozens of them, each an aberrant mixture of all the races of Evil and Chaos. In some ways they resembled Orcs; in others they resembled Trolls or Lizard Men. Yet for each point of likeness there were a

dozen points of difference. Some had hides which
gleamed like burnished steel and brass. Others had human
faces gaping from their stomachs. Some had feathers and
great crests, some flapped bat-wings or padded forward
on cat-paws or goat-hoofs. One had an arm that ended
in two cobras, which it snapped like a whip. Another
was as large as a bear, its pulsing inner organs visible
through its translucent skin. There were Siamese twins
joined at the hip which had the faces of beautiful women
and the fangs of poisonous serpents. Some crawled on
caterpillar bodies as large as horses. One had a human
face leering out from the body of a spider. It was a
parade of abominations such as might drive any decent
human being to madness, and their hideous appearance
was not the worst of it.

Far more terrifying, the mutant creatures flowed and
changed as they grew. Just as the eye was becoming
accustomed to one nightmare shape, it would pulse and
re-form into something even worse. A body would
extend grasping pseudopods, arms would become leech-
mouthed tentacles or clicking pincer-claws. Legs would
flow together and the body would slide earthwards till it
had become the huge orange torso of a giant slug,
gliding forward on a trail of poisonous slime. Everywhere
the various forms of life twisted into being, then adapted
into another shape. Nothing remained constant.

The smell was indescribably vile, making all three
onlookers retch and gag. The cacophony of sound the
creatures unleashed echoed round the cavern until Yaztromo feared for his eardrums.

'We're dead,' Weasel shouted with finality.

'While I live I will fight!' Darkmane replied.

Yaztromo couldn't help but notice the flat note of
fatalism in his voice. Once more he searched within

himself for his reserves of magical power, trying to scrape together some last vestiges of his inner resources for a spell. He had managed to bleed a little power from the Bloodstone and since then he had stopped feeling so weak. As he had half suspected, the thing had been draining his energies vampirically. Perhaps, given a few moments' peace, he could start pulling some back . . .

Too late! The mass of mutants surged forward irresistibly. Paralysing tendrils lashed out, forcing Darkmane, in the lead, to leap back. Somewhere, something that sounded like a mastodon trumpeted in triumph. Suddenly the creatures halted in their advance. A deafening silence fell over the chamber.

'Magnificent, are they not?' a surprisingly polite voice enquired. 'And rather attractive, if in an overstated sort of way.'

Yaztromo turned and saw a foppish form leaning in the chamber's open doorway. It stroked its narrow chin thoughtfully with one slender hand. Yaztromo recognized the presence of the despoiler of Drystone.

Darkmane turned to regard him, midnight-black eyes blazing with fury. 'What do you want?' he asked.

'Nothing,' Cawlis replied. 'I just thought I would give you a moment to admire my creations before they kill you. I admit to being human enough to be proud of my handiwork. Well, you have had your moment of aesthetic contemplation. Pray continue with your deaths!'

He clapped his hands, and the mutant creatures advanced once more. Deep within himself, however, Yaztromo had seized the moment's respite to focus a spell. He uttered the words that resonated round the chamber like thunderclaps. Whips of lightning lashed out from his hands.

Cawlis dived back through the arch to avoid them,

but his foul creations were not so lucky. The stink of scorched flesh and ozone filled the air. The mutants retreated, but not before Yaztromo observed that their hides were becoming thicker and more rubbery.

'Hurry,' he panted. 'The effect of my spell will not last for long.'

They made a rush for the stairs.

'Still got a few tricks left then, old man!' Weasel grinned with relief.

Yaztromo nodded. *Maybe two more spells,* he thought, *then I am finally finished.*

'Up!' roared Darkmane. 'We must reach the balloon!'

19

Away

Darkmane spun on his heel and slammed the doorbolt into place. From the other side came the sound of hammering as their pursuers tried to break through. The door bulged under the impact of their savage blows but it did not give way.

'That won't hold them for long,' Weasel cried. His face was twisted with fear and he still panted from the effort of the long climb. He looked as if he had aged twenty years in the space of a few scant hours.

'Thanks for reminding me,' Darkmane snarled, snatching up his sword. In his hand, still wrapped in Weasel's scarf, the Bloodstone glowed brighter still, its sickening radiance seeming to burn right through the cloth. Strange patterns of light danced across the adventurers' faces. In that moment, seeing them illuminated by the witchfire of the gem, Darkmane had an eerie premonition. Suddenly, somehow, he knew in his bones that one of them was not going to survive this night. He reassured himself that it was simply the jewel's evil influence that was making him think that way – but he could not make himself believe it.

Away

He feared most for Yaztromo. The old man was bent almost double, his breath rasping in his chest. Leaning heavily on his staff for support, he looked almost too old and feeble to continue. Vermithrax stood in front of his master, watching him dolefully with bright, beady eyes.

'Not as young as I used to be, eh, my pet?' the magician gasped, forcing a wan smile. He turned to the door and considered the bulging timbers. 'Once I could have bound that portal with a spell. Now . . .' he spread his hands helplessly. 'I must save my strength for the last resort.'

The sound of light feet came rushing along the corridor towards them.

Vermithrax fluttered his wings in panic. 'Yaaaz! Goberlings! C-rawk! Danger! Danger!'

A horde of the small creatures burst into the room through the unbarred exit.

Darkmane glared at them and smiled grimly. 'They are mine,' he said. He strode among them and flickering death was in his hand.

On the other side of the bolted door, a writhing, mewling mass of creatures fought to get through. Orcs of Cawlis's personal bodyguard wrestled with tentacled monstrosities freshly erupted from the pods. Their bodies were packed so tight that none could move properly, let alone get an effective swing at the door.

'Form up! Form up!' yelled the Troll commander, using his enormous strength to beat a path forward. He brought his axe-haft crashing down on the head of one of the mutants. Its skull fractured with a sickening crunch . . . then the jelly of its brain started to ooze round the splinters of bone and the whole thing began to knit together again. The Orcs struggled to assemble themselves into some sort of formation and, swords at the ready, began to push through the mutants towards the doorway.

All at once the Troll leader heard a new clamour of shouts and yells coming from behind him. Turning, he froze on the spot. Forcing its way through the ramshackle mob was a figure out of his most private, lonely nightmares. It was Axion, horn-headed, glowing-eyed, a great hole gaping in his chest cavity, crumbling grey skin drifting off in immense flakes. He ignored the jaws that tore away gobbets of his flesh. Mutating tentacles reached out for him, but he shrugged them off with awesome strength. His taloned hands were bludgeons. Whenever he landed a blow the victim fell, stunned.

Even as the Troll watched, the undead sorcerer ripped the head from an Orc then the arm from a Lizard Man. He flailed around with this bloody club, inexorably forcing his way forward.

'Let me through!' cried his anguished voices, crazed with blood-lust and pain and grief. 'The Bloodstone is mine! It is me! I must have it! Out of my way!'

Fearfully, the Troll stepped aside to let him pass.

Axion confronted the door for a moment. He drew back one fist. A blow like a battering ram landed against the timbers and the door exploded, splinters of wood and iron flying everywhere.

The dam holding back the wave of bodies broke. Battle-crazed soldiers and mutants swarmed past the screaming creature. The Troll was unsure whether they were pursuing their prey or were simply fleeing from Axion, but it mattered little. The way was now clear; he would catch the intruders and regain the favour of his master . . . or he would die trying.

*

Away

Darkmane burst through the last doorway and into the cold night air. It was good to feel the clean, fresh chill again. He had begun to wonder whether they would ever escape the noisome depths.

Star was standing beside the basket of Elumbar's deflated balloon. Turning at his arrival, she gasped at the sight of him. He grinned; he had to admit he was probably not a pretty picture, bespattered as he was with the remains of his enemies.

'Chadda, I was so worried!' she cried. 'What is that noise?'

'We are pursued. Quickly, light the brazier! We must away!'

Yaztromo stumbled into view. His breath stuttered out in clouds of condensation. 'Just a moment . . . Hamaskis, my heart! I don't think it can stand much more of this!'

'I don't think my guts can stand much more of this,' Weasel added, bounding past the wizard as if all the devils of the pit were at his heels. 'Hello, you pretty baggage! Miss me? How about a kiss for the returning heroes, then? You won't believe what we've seen.'

'No time for that!' Darkmane scowled. 'Help Star light the brazier. We must be off!'

'First sensible thing you've said all night,' Weasel said, but not so loud that Darkmane could hear.

'We don't have time,' said Yaztromo. 'They are coming up the stairs even as I speak. And what's that over there? How did *they* get here?'

Coming round the corner of the nearest tower was a squad of Orcs and Goblins. *They must have been waiting for us*, Darkmane thought. *How could they have got so close without Star noticing?* He grasped his notched blade, readying himself for the inevitable attack.

'Hold them off while I prepare a spell!' Yaztromo shouted.

'Get into the balloon, you old fool. You're in no state to cast anything. Put your faith in cold steel for once. It'll save us.'

Seeing that Darkmane showed no fear, the Orcs had slowed. That was bad, he thought; it showed some tactical sense. They fanned out in a half-circle before advancing again. Darkmane leapt among them, sweeping his trusty sword in a mighty arc, sending one Orc head flying and caving in another's ribs. The others circled him, searching for an opening. Cat quick, Darkmane feinted a strike at one, then rammed his blade into another's stomach. It fell to the ground. He moved to put his back to the wall of the battlements, hoping that they would concentrate on him and not take this opportunity to rush the balloon.

Another Orc warrior skipped in at him. Twisting to avoid his scimitar, Darkmane's foot slipped in a pool of blood and the creature was inside his guard. He regained his balance just in time to duck a blow that would have removed his head from his shoulders. He sidestepped, and the Orc went past him. Darkmane lashed out with a back-kick that sent it tumbling over the battlements. Its screams faded slowly as it fell out of earshot.

To his surprise Darkmane noticed that Weasel had leapt out of the balloon and had come to his aid. The little man managed to put his blade through an Orc's back, then he stepped forward to join Darkmane. He glanced at the warrior.

'Be a while before that balloon goes anywhere, mate — and if you fall it won't be going nowhere. Anyway I've got to look good in front of the girl, you know what I mean?'

Away

Their inhuman opponents had regrouped; now they were advancing all together. Blades flashing, Darkmane and Weasel fought, back to back, until they were surrounded by a wall of fallen Orcs and Goblins. Bleeding from a dozen small cuts, Darkmane risked a glance at the balloon. It was now nearly inflated and was drifting slowly upwards. Yaztromo was in the basket, along with Star. The Elf girl was frantically dumping ballast over the side. Darkmane watched as the balloon rose to about a man's height above the ground. Now it was held in place only by the rope mooring it to one of the ruined turrets.

At that moment more of the enemy arrived, clambering up the stairwell. Slowly the landing area started to fill with them, and they formed up for a charge.

'Oops!' Weasel muttered. Darkmane knew there were too many to fight and, surrounded as they were, they would not be able to reach the balloon. Darkmane prepared to sell his life dearly.

Axion stalked the dark corridors below Hellsgate Keep, as he had done so many centuries before, and memories flooded back. From here he had once ruled an empire. Now it was the stronghold of his enemy. He felt weak, the Bloodstone was at a distance now and his spirit was split between it and this new body. He knew he must regain it if he was to have any control over his destiny. For too long he had danced like a puppet at the end of Cawlis's strings. Rage and anguish filled his heart, but he had mastered the emotions to do his bidding.

He swept past piles of dead bodies and understood where a battle had raged. The ones he pursued were mighty warriors: they had slain many times their number and had not succumbed. That was good; it meant that the Bloodstone had not yet fallen into the hands of his foe.

He entered the hall that had once been his throne room and paused for a moment. It seemed a cold and hollow place, this, the former seat of his power. *So passes all worldly glory, crippled by time*, he thought to himself.

Cawlis rose from the shadows of the throne. He was a small, pale figure. When he spoke, his voice was calm, polite and almost obsequious. Axion knew now just how deceptive that voice was.

'Good evening, my Lord Axion,' Cawlis trilled.

'Out of my way!' Axion grated, moving closer and flexing his talons.

'Such bad manners,' Cawlis tutted. 'It pains me to say it, but there's nothing I deplore more.'

'I care not for your feelings, creature. I will deal with you now,' said Axion, the voice of his anger dominant in the chorus. He reached out and grasped the other's wrist with one petrified claw. As if joining a dance Cawlis grasped the wrist of Axion's free hand.

'You are a fool,' said Axion. 'You have attuned yourself to the Bloodstone and used its power in the creation of your creatures. If the thieves master it, they will destroy you as well as me. You have left traces of your true self within its aura. They will know you truly, as I do.'

'You are old, Axion, alive long after your time. You do not know me. You hardly even know yourself any more.' There was no trace of strain in Cawlis's voice, although both of them were involved in a contest of superhuman strength. Almost casually, he forced the animated corpse to its knees. With a twist of his wrist he broke off Axion's hand.

'So sad,' he said. 'You used to call yourself Axion, Master of Shadows. Now you are hardly even master of your own crumbling body. When I have reclaimed the

Bloodstone I will deal with you finally and for ever. I will give you immortality, fool: the immortality of the grave.'

He turned on his heel and left Axion kneeling before his former throne. If tears could have flowed from his jewelled eyes, Axion would have wept.

Darkmane looked out over the sea of twisted faces and heard scores of voices howling for his blood. The Bloodstone pulsed in his left hand; his blade hung heavy in his right. He knew that in a few seconds his life would be over. His premonition had come true, as he knew it must.

He turned to take a last look at Star and Yaztromo before the monsters overwhelmed him entirely. He saw the old wizard complete a mystical pass and heard him utter a strangled incantation. Lines of white-blue force flashed from his fingers and a wall of shimmering energy swept through the enemy, driving them to one side, away from the balloon and away from Darkmane. The path was clear.

'Go!' Darkmane bellowed. Weasel needed no further urging. The two men sprinted for the balloon and swarmed up the line.

'Hurry! I cannot hold this spell much longer.'

Darkmane swarmed aboard the gondola just as Weasel dropped over the other side of the basket. Behind Darkmane the blue glow faded.

'Here they come!' cried Star.

'Quickly, Weasel! Cut the line! Cut the line!' Darkmane ordered. Weasel leaned out and began to saw at the rope with his blade. Darkmane watched as the monstrous regiment advanced, a green tide threatening to swarm up the ruined spire and overwhelm the balloon. *It's going to be close*, he thought.

*

It's going to be close, too close! Yaztromo thought. The little brazier Elumbar had provided would not provide sufficient heat to lift them clear, even now that all the ballast was gone.

Vermithrax fluttered round the balloon. 'Yaaaz! Yaaaz!' he cawed. An arrow whizzed by him and he flapped away to safety behind the balloon.

Barely strong enough to keep his eyes open, Yaztromo began what he knew would be his final spell. The strain of the past few hours had been so very great and fatigue had almost overcome him. No! He was not going to give up now. Perhaps Darkmane was right after all: there should be heroes. He spoke the words of the incantation and his fist burst into flames. He took a risk and directed a great jet of it into the gas-bag, hoping that the fabric would not catch fire. The balloon strained against the anchoring rope.

'Cut it! Cut it!' Star screamed.

'I'm trying to!' Weasel shouted in reply.

The Lizard Men and Orcs were upon them. Some tried to clamber up the mooring rope while others scrambled up the rubble of the tower. Unable to keep his balance, one Lizard Man fell, only to be replaced by another.

The rope gave way! The balloon leapt skyward then jerked to a halt. The creatures had formed a chain and were holding the gondola down. Darkmane leaned out of the basket and hacked at them, one-handed, with his sword. The craft was swaying precariously in the air. Realizing he had to get a better grip on his sword, Darkmane turned and tossed the Bloodstone to Star. As it looped through the air, it became separated from Weasel's scarf.

'Catch it,' Darkmane cried. Grasping his blade in a

two-handed grip, he hewed at the nearest Orc. It fell back, screaming, and the restraining chain broke. The balloon rose, unfettered, into the sky.

Below them, their enemies howled with frustration. Hanging on to the edge of the gondola, Darkmane looked down and grinned in triumph. They were free!

Behind him, Darkmane heard Star's sudden agonized scream.

'No!' she cried. Her hands had gone up reflexively and caught the Bloodstone; now she was holding it as if it were burning her.

He turned to see what was ailing Star — and his heart leapt.

20

Clouds and Claws

The baleful light of the Bloodstone lit Star's twisted face from below. She screamed an animal yowl as her clothes shredded. Spines erupted from her back and her form began to twist and alter. Her fingers became taloned claws. Her jaw elongated, and massive teeth slid down into her gaping mouth. Great spurs of bone jutted out through her torn breeches. Her back seemed to contract so that she hunched forward. A great crest of spines erupted from her skull as the hair retracted into her scalp.

'The Bloodstone is mine now, humans. My master will reward me well!' Was it just Darkmane's imagination, or was there an element of regret in the look the monster gave him?

'That damned jewel, it's changed her into a monster,' Weasel cried.

'No,' Yaztromo contradicted him. 'She shares the same maker. Like has transformed like. Her true form is revealed at last.'

Weasel leapt forward and tried to wrestle the gem from the grasp of the thing that had been Star. The

211

creature knocked him flying with a single back-handed buffet. He lay, sprawled on the floor of the basket, groaning and clutching his face.

Darkmane could not stand idly by. He sheathed his blade and dived on her, holding her wrists and trying to force her claws open. At the same time, Yaztromo lashed out at her with his staff. It was like hitting a brick wall. The balloon's basket swayed from side to side.

Darkmane gazed into the creature's eyes and smelled its fetid breath. His mind was in turmoil. Was this really Star, the girl he had saved in the woods? Had she always been this . . . this thing? Her tongue lashed out and licked his face. He felt a dribble of saliva trickle down.

'What's the matter, Chadda?' she mocked. 'Do my kisses not please you? Does the sight of the real me disturb you?' Horrifyingly, the voice was still Star's. To think that this creature had been among them all the time. Was this the true reason it had wanted to get him alone; to take him by surprise and devour him? His mind reeled at the implications of it all.

Momentarily his physical grasp weakened and the thing broke free. It scrambled on to the side of the basket and squatted there for a moment, the glowing Bloodstone clutched in one taloned claw.

'Goodbye, all!' It grinned and allowed itself to fall backwards out of the gondola.

'Star! No!' Darkmane screamed.

'There never was any Star,' said Yaztromo quietly. 'They often take such fair forms. Doubtless poor Celanion was fooled the same way, before she led him to her mate. The one you killed.'

'No,' said Darkmane. 'No!'

He clambered over the side of the basket, grabbed a rope and hurled himself out into space.

'Don't jump!' Weasel shouted. 'It's not that bad. Wait a minute! What about my money?'

The basket jerked as Darkmane's weight pulled the rope taut. Looking over the side, Weasel saw Darkmane's face looking up at him. In the new light of the fresh-breaking dawn he could see the torment in Darkmane's eyes.

'Take us down lower!' Darkmane called.

'He's mad, he is,' said Weasel. 'Better do as he says.'

Darkmane watched the tree-covered hills rise rapidly to meet him. His heart was full of fury – and an aching sense of loss. Down there was the Star-thing. It had the Bloodstone, which he and the others had risked their lives for, and it intended to return it to the master of Hellsgate. That he would not, could not, allow. The creature had deceived him, made a fool of him, made him believe that it was something worth caring for. Black rage filled him, driving him to the edge of madness. He wanted revenge.

The treetops were centimetres below him now. He thought he saw a grim, monstrous shape loping through the shadows below. By the time the flying machine touched down it would be gone. There was only one thing to do: he let go of the rope.

As he fell, he was reminded of the time he had leapt from Zharradan Marr's flying ship. Had he really been rescued by a goddess? Or was that simply a pain-induced hallucination, brought on by his injuries? Yaztromo had never told him the truth. No man could visit the realm of the gods, could they?

Leaves whipped past his face; branches lashed his body. The breath was battered from him as he made contact with the tops of the trees. Frantically he tried to snatch at a branch, in order to break his fall. His fingers closed on one and his arm was nearly ripped from its socket. The sudden pain made him let go and he fell once more, tumbling through the air towards the ground.

'Ouch! That looks painful!' Weasel commented as he watched Darkmane vanish among the leaves. The trickster shook his head. One thing you could always say about old Darkmane – he never took the easy route anywhere.

Weasel rubbed his own aching ribs; he'd been putting up with quite a lot of pain recently. It must be starting to affect his mind – why else had he risked joining Darkmane on the battlements? Had some of the big maniac's stupid heroism started to rub off on him? Somehow, during the long night in the caverns, he had experienced so much fear that it no longer really bothered him. His capacity for terror seemed to have drained out of him and he had discovered a certain courage within himself. Maybe he really was becoming a hero! Weasel certainly hoped not. Real heroes tended to have very short lives.

He turned to look at the wizard. Yaztromo was slumped over the tiller, the flame gone from his hand. He looked old and pale and drawn.

'What now, Yazz?' Weasel asked.

'We bring this confounded contraption down somehow, of course. We must find them both!'

'I was afraid you were going to say that.'

21

In the Forest

Star dragged herself towards consciousness. Slowly she
rose to her feet. How long had she been out? No way of
telling. The Bloodstone? Still clutched in one taloned
paw, thank the Dark Maker. Cawlis would have the skin
flayed from her if she lost it now. She inspected her
ridged and armoured body for injuries. Not too bad!
Some bruising, a few tender patches, the odd broken
spur of bone. She would heal, in time.

Strange how things went, really. All she had wanted
was a decent meal. That stupid Elf, Celanion, would have
done – only Darkmane and his companions had to
interfere. They'd even killed Grimble, and he'd been
tough, even for a Shapechanger. It had seemed best to
go along with the deception then. Particularly with that
suspicious old wizard present, curse his ancient bones.
She would like to have cracked open his femur and
sucked out the marrow. She had had high hopes that she
could have lured Darkmane outside and taken him off
guard in an intimate moment. Who would have thought
he would play so hard to get? He'd become a challenge
really; that's why she'd concentrated on him rather than

216

on Weasel. He was too easy, far too easy. Not too much meat on that stringy frame either — and could you just imagine the taste?

She knew she'd been stupid agreeing to go to the castle, but she had thought there might have been a chance of picking off Darkmane or the wizard there. If only she hadn't gone hunting that plump little Goblin; they'd never have caught her and she'd never have met Cawlis. Now there was a scary one: so polite and quiet, yet so threatening. He was unlike any shape-shifter Star had ever met, even though he claimed to be one. She'd believed his threats, though — and his promises.

If they escape, stay with them, he'd said — no, promised. What he said would be. You're my insurance against them getting away, my spy in their camp, as it were. A canny one, that, too. Star found that to be quite an attractive quality. Perhaps he'd make an even better mate than Grimble, who, for all his good qualities, had been quite stupid. It was a good plan — and it would have worked, too, if that imbecile Darkmane hadn't tossed her the jewel, forcing her to revert to her true shape.

She shook her head to clear some of the fog that still lurked around in the corners of her vision. Perhaps even that was for the best. All she had to do now was to get the stone back to Lord Cawlis. Maybe he would take a shine to her after that.

She sensed rather than saw the presence. One second it wasn't there, the next it was looming over her. It was tall and horned and its eyes were glowing gems. It had only one good hand, which was stretched towards her.

'Give me my Bloodstone,' five separate voices said simultaneously. Star sprang back, away from its grasp. She snarled at Axion, baring her fangs. Somehow, she could tell it wasn't at all impressed.

'Give me the Bloodstone, child,' it said. 'What I once made I can unmake.'

There was a sense of threat about its words that scared Star, even though she didn't understand them. The word 'Axion' reverberated through the dimmest corners of her brain, ancestral memories rising into the light of day.

'You want it? Take it!' She threw the Bloodstone at him. It bounced off his horned head in a shower of crimson sparks. He fell heavily to the ground . . . and then, ever so slowly, Axion began to crawl towards where the Bloodstone lay.

'C-rawk! Nice landing!' Vermithrax screeched as they pulled themselves from the wreckage of the gondola. 'Land on your brains, did you?'

Weasel picked himself up and inspected the new additions to his growing collection of bruises. He rubbed his aching behind. He had known it would be a ridiculous idea to land a balloon in the middle of the forest, but would that stupid wizard listen? No chance! Everyone always knew better than Weasel. Well, he wasn't one to hold a grudge, not when his cash was still at stake.

'You know something, Yazz,' he said conversationally as he helped the wizard to his feet. 'I really fancied my chances with that Star. I could tell by the way she looked at me, I thought. She had a kind of hungry look in her eye, know what I mean? That'll teach me to think twice when it comes to women, eh?'

'I suppose so,' said Yaztromo, who wasn't really interested. They both froze at the sound of the yell.

'You don't think . . .'

'We'd best investigate,' Yaztromo decided. They made

as swift progress as they could through the undergrowth in the direction of the sound.

Axion reached out for the Bloodstone. It was practically within his grasp . . . so close . . . just a little further. His claw was almost touching it when it was kicked out of his reach. He looked up, into the bruised and angry face of a tall, raven-haired human clad in the tattered remains of black armour.

'You shall not have it again, fiend,' said Darkmane. His body ached beyond all tolerance, and wherever his skin was exposed it had been lacerated by the bushes which had eventually absorbed the main force of his fall. Once he had fled this creature in terror. Now he was so angry that there was no room for any other emotion.

Axion lurched to his feet and swung the stump of his arm. Darkmane tried to dodge, but the fall had slowed his reflexes considerably. The blow caught him on the jaw and sent him reeling. An involuntary cry escaped his lips.

Golden stars danced before his eyes. He lashed out with his boot and caught the sorcerer between the legs. A mortal man would have been stunned by such a blow but Axion shrugged it off; he simply picked the warrior up and hurled him against a tree. Darkness threatened to overwhelm Darkmane. In his fading vision he saw Axion pick up the gem. *No! Not to come this far and fail at the last*, he urged himself. He forced himself to move. To fight.

He staggered over to the sorcerer. Axion was clutching the Bloodstone in his one good hand, holding it high above his head. He seemed to be bathed in its pulsating radiance. Darkmane reached up to take the evil artefact and began to pull the sorcerer's hand down. Too late, he

In the Forest

realized that this was exactly what Axion intended. The mage thrust the gem against Darkmane's brow. White fire danced in knives through his destroyed brain.

Yaztromo and Weasel burst heavily into the forest glade. Before them lay the recumbent forms of Darkmane and Axion, sprawled on the ground a few metres apart. Between them lay the sinisterly glowing Bloodstone. Yaztromo's heart sank when he saw his young friend's still form. Could Darkmane really be dead?

Weasel's heart did not sink — until the moment when Star sprang into the clearing. She looked more battered than the last time he had seen her, but she was still so very swift and dangerous. Her claws flexed. 'The stone is mine!' she hissed triumphantly.

'I don't think so,' Weasel said nervously, still advancing, his blade held ready. 'I don't think it's anybody's, really. It's been nothing but trouble in actual fact. Look at us: we've had no end of bother since we found it. Chased by sorcerers and Orcs and Trolls, crashed balloons, had our best girl turn into a ravening monster. The blinking thing's cursed, I tell you. It's not meant for . . . people, yes, people like you and me. Best leave it to the experts . . . like Yaztromo there.'

All the while, as he spoke, he edged closer and closer to the gem. Seeing through his game, Star leapt at him, lashing out with a claw. He ducked back out of reach.

'Aw, come on, Star! After all we've meant to each other, you don't really want to hurt me, do you?'

She sprang forward again. Weasel raised his blade in front of him and she had to spring back to avoid being impaled. He could easily have pressed home his advantage and injured her then if he had wanted to, simply by leaning forward, but something, perhaps the memory of the innocent girl she had once seemed to be, stayed his hand.

'Look, I know you're not really a monster. It was that sorcerer changed you. I understand. We can find a way to change you back. Old Yaztromo's a wizard. He knows about these things. With the power of the Bloodstone, well, he could have you right as rain in a . . .'

This time she came in under his guard, knocking him to the ground. She'd expected him to be weak, but Weasel was all stringy muscle and tough bone. Driven by fear now, a desperate, desperate fear, he was surprisingly powerful; and she was weak, she found. Her long fall must have taken more out of her than she had thought. They rolled over and over on the ground while Star tried to rake Weasel with her talons. He ignored the scratches. Whenever she saw an opening, she tried to bite at his throat but, somehow, he always managed to wriggle out of her way.

Inexorably Weasel was gaining the upper hand. With a final roll, he was astride the Star-creature's chest, his dagger against her throat. 'Don't make me kill you, girl. Don't!' he pleaded.

A shadow fell across them both. Weasel looked up and winced. 'Er . . . I wasn't actually going to hurt her, your sorcererness,' he said, gazing up into the tranquil face of Cawlis.

'I do so appreciate that,' said Cawlis. His almost perfunctory back-handed slap sent Weasel flying across the clearing, to land in a crumpled heap.

Star looked up at him with a smile as false as any she had ever given. 'Master, help me. I have the stone!'

Cawlis stamped his foot down on her neck. There was terrible power in his slender leg and it broke her bones like so many dried twigs. 'I've never liked liars,' he said mildly.

In the Forest

Something snapped in Weasel: it was the very casual way Cawlis had killed her after all Weasel's attempts to spare her; the one time he had tried to show anyone mercy in his life and this . . . this monster had spoiled it!

'I'm going to KILL YOU!' he howled, charging at the gaunt figure.

'Oh, don't be tiresome,' his opponent sighed, ducking under his blow effortlessly. Weasel sailed past. Cawlis shook his head sadly. 'Humans. I don't know. They always have to make the heroic gesture, don't they?'

'Stand still and fight, damn you,' Weasel grated.

'You mean like this?' Cawlis's fist lashed out, too quickly for the eye to follow. Weasel's ribs snapped. He looked down, to see bone protruding from his chest.

'Or do you mean like this?' Cawlis lifted him as if he were weightless. Weasel watched the ground recede below him. Cawlis's pale, lean face smiled pleasantly up at him as he held him aloft. Then the ground came up to meet him. Hard. Weasel blacked out for a moment. Silver shards of agony ran through his nerves like so many spears of ice.

'Or perhaps you mean like this.' Cawlis's kick smashed into Weasel's broken ribs. Screaming agony brought him back to consciousness.

Cawlis turned and walked away from his foe's recumbent body. As if looking on from a distance, Weasel watched the booted feet retreat. He knew he was dying. It just wasn't fair. Why did it have to be so painful? This wasn't the way a Weasel died!

By sheer effort of will he forced himself to his feet. He stood upright and drew in a breath. His chest felt like a furnace. His vision had narrowed until it was just a dark tunnel with Cawlis at the far end of it.

'Come back!' Weasel tried to shout, though his voice

came out as little more than a whisper. 'I haven't finished with you yet.'

Cawlis strode confidently back towards the tottering Weasel. The little man struggled to lift his blade. It felt as if it weighed a ton, but slowly he managed to get it aloft.

Cawlis stood in front of him and looked deep into his eyes. Nothing was reflected there. 'Amazing. What bravery. Bravo!' he mocked.

Weasel fell over backwards. He was already dead.

Cawlis glanced nonchalantly round the glade. It was all over, and so easily, too. His triumph was complete. Now where was the Bloodstone?

'Is this what you're looking for?' asked Yaztromo, his voice full of a terrible rage.

22

Elsewhen

White fire blazed through Darkmane's brain; lightning rippled through every molecule of his being.

He tumbled, head over heels, through infinity. As he fell, he stretched, clutching out for anything solid, but he did not encounter anything. As Darkmane tumbled through the void, the pain wracking his tired body vanished, to be replaced by a cold, electric tingling. Still he fell through chasms of infinite shadows and down wells of solidified light.

The shadows shifted. Monstrous faces loomed round him: old enemies, old friends; all subtly distorted. He lived scenes from his most ancient memories: of his castle and his laboratory, of his earliest experiments and greatest triumphs; he built and toppled empires. He married and saw his first child still-born, and resolved that never again would death take anything from him.

Slowly it dawned on him that these were not *his* memories; this was not *his* life – he was living through the recollections of a stranger. Most of what he was experiencing was simply beyond his comprehension. He dreamed of a shadow-life and was drowning in unfamiliar sensation. It corroded the boundaries of his self, threatening to wash away the core of what he was beneath a tide of ultimate otherness.

No! He was Chadda Darkmane, chosen by the gods themselves to perform great deeds. He was a warrior in the service of Salamon, of truth and of justice. He lived to gain Amonour. He was a simple man, a man of action, a doer of deeds. He did not experiment on innocents; he did not animate corpses or create corrupt monsters. He did not crave oblivion and a release from guilt with every fibre of his being. With every newly remembered assertion, a part of his memories of otherness faded. He felt more solid, more concrete, more real; finally, he became himself once more.

He stood alone, enveloped in a blood-red mist. Within the fog faces drifted, large as a man, monsters, figments of another's imagination. In search of a constant, he lifted his hand in front of his face. It seemed real to him, made of solid flesh and sinew. As his eyes strayed up his wrist, Darkmane realized that he was naked – and in that moment he suddenly became fully clothed.

What madness is this, he wondered; *is this death? If so, it is like no heaven or hell I have ever heard tell of.* He began to walk through the mist, and it was as if he was pushing against a treadmill. No matter how many paces he took, he never got anywhere.

Sometimes, from the mist, unfamiliar voices rang out around him. Their words were fragments, half-forgotten memories: declarations of love and hate, pleadings and ravings and puzzled enquiries. They ranged from whispers to echoes louder than thunder. Darkmane did his best to ignore them, but his mind was in sore need of solid ground.

The pungent smell of ammonia filled the air, closely

followed by a memory of the scent of newly cut grass. It was replaced by the smell of a woman's perfume – roses, so many roses – then the overpowering aroma of decaying corpses and of surgical spirit.

'Where am I?' Darkmane shouted in confusion. His words echoed away into the distance, repeating themselves thousands of times, never quite fading away into silence.

After a lifetime of echoes, something responded: 'Within the Bloodstone.'

Darkmane wasn't sure whether it was one voice or five. Each word seemed to be spoken by a different voice, repeated a fraction of a second later by the others. The words wrapped and entwined around one another, surrounding Darkmane in a cacophony of voices.

'Show yourself,' he demanded. 'Face me like a true warrior! Do not hide amid these phantasms and illusions!'

Suddenly, as if it had always been, it was there: a horned skull floating at head height. Bejewelled eyes stared from it. Five talons hovered where a hand should have been. A withered claw hung in the mist as if attached to an invisible arm. Where a heart should have been, the Bloodstone pulsed wickedly. There was no body, just the hint of an outline in the swirling mist. 'Phantasms and illusions?' the five voices twisted out the words. 'Yes, I suppose you are correct; that IS what my life has become.'

The thing made no move to threaten him, but Darkmane was still wary. 'Where am I? Speak truth, creature, or it will be the worse for you!'

Axion's laughter was not mocking, simply tainted with a hint of sadness. 'Within the heart of the Bloodstone. Within a dream. Within my own dream. Take your pick, mortal – all are to some extent true.'

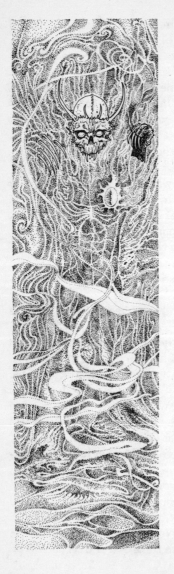

'You speak in riddles. Curse all sorcerers; can you not speak clear and true? I want an explanation, not further riddles. This is no game.'

'This is no simple thing, Chadda Darkmane – yes, I know you, as you know me – and simple words will not reveal it all. The Bloodstone is the refuge of my soul. It is the store of my memories and the essence of my long-forgotten power. I created it as a last retreat, a final, unassailable fortress where my spirit could reside if ever my body was destroyed. In the end, I knew I could not escape death in the real world, so I removed myself to a world within myself. Alas, I wrought this new world too well. I have spent centuries in the most solitary of confinements, locked away with my memories. And I have so many bad memories, Chadda Darkmane . . .'

'I have seen some.' Darkmane shivered as uncommon emotions swept through him.

'Then perhaps you can imagine how I felt. Trapped, with no company but the creations of my own imagination, with endless years to ponder my actions and eventually learn the true meaning of guilt.'

'I would go mad if I had done what you have done,' Darkmane heard himself say.

'I did go mad. I went mad many times. I may still be mad and this may be a rare moment of lucidity. It may yet be one last moment of insanity. I can no longer judge.'

'But you control this world. It is shaped by your imagination. Could you not distract yourself, lose yourself among your dreams?'

'Ah yes! Here I have power limited only by my imagination. I have conquered imaginary

kingdoms and overcome imaginary foes. I have committed acts of unspeakable degeneracy and made illusory repentance for my crimes. But imagination is ultimately limited, Chadda Darkmane, and I have found the limits of mine. When at last all distractions failed, memory returned to haunt me. I was trapped in a prison of my own making, and I could not escape.'

Darkmane considered the sorcerer. He could see that Axion's appearance had deceived him; the sorcerer was no real threat to anyone. Unless, that is, this was all some elaborately subtle trap, a spider's web of illusions meant to turn Darkmane's mind to some unfathomable purpose.

'Yet you came back – to Titan.'

'I was summoned by Cawlis.' When Axion spoke the Shapechanger's name, the mists became agitated by unseen forces. Lightning flashed in the distance, to be answered by the faint rumble of thunder. 'Yes; scheming, subtle Cawlis. His destiny is interconnected with the Bloodstone now, though he knows it not. He has used its power, sacrificed himself to it. He created a channel to draw on its power, but channels flow in both directions.'

'Surely he is but a shape-shifter,' Darkmane ventured, 'albeit an uncommonly powerful one.'

'Oh no, Chadda Darkmane, you too have succumbed to his illusion. He is so much more than that. No mere shape-shifter could have brought me back or bound me, or made me reveal my secrets.'

The tone of Axion's voices had changed, Darkmane noticed. The sad voice was fading, the angry voice becoming dominant.

'This Cawlis brought you back?'

'Oh yes, he brought me back. He wanted my secrets;

he wanted an invincible army and the power of the Bloodstone. He brought me back in order to use my knowledge, deliberately to make the same mistakes I had unwillingly made in my ignorance and blind arrogant folly.'

'You gave him the knowledge to create those monsters? I would have died first.'

'You speak too easily of death, Chadda Darkmane.' Axion's voice held a note of wild fury. Darkmane could sense that its sanity was receding. 'All you have ever done is to vouchsafe death to those whom you deemed deserving of it. You have delivered so much death, yet you know so very little of what you deliver. Hear me now: you must know whereof you speak before you pass judgement on ME!'

Flesh flowed once more through Axion's outline. He became solid, powerful, tangible. He advanced towards Darkmane, bejewelled eyes flashing.

23

Face-off

Yaztromo rested wearily on his staff, the Bloodstone throbbing in his right hand, a continual reminder of his predicament. He was at the very end of his strength, more tired than any mortal had a right to be and remain alive; but he let no trace of his weakness show in his face or his voice. He knew that to do so would spell the end, for him, for Darkmane, for all the innocent souls between this accursed forest glade and distant Salamonis. He knew that, if he allowed Cawlis any opening, the Shapechanger would pounce.

His opponent was a picture of relaxation. He stood nonchalantly over Darkmane's body, inspecting his clean fingernails with a critical eye as if not the slightest particle of dirt would possibly escape his gaze.

'You look tired, old man,' he said almost solicitously. From the tone of his quiet, cultured voice it would be impossible to guess that he had just brutally slain two sentient creatures. 'Perhaps you would like to rest. It would hardly be sporting of me to kill a man who needs a stick to get around, now would it? Why don't you just give me the Bloodstone, there's a good fellow, and that will be the end of the matter. You have my word on it. What do you say?'

'I'm not tired enough to fall for your smooth talk, monster, or to let my guard down for an instant.' Yaztromo could feel the magic surging within the Bloodstone, as if it knew that the creature who wished to enslave its arcane powers was present. If only he could find a way to tap its power as he had before, but he was tired, so very tired . . .

'How bothersome.' Cawlis might have been talking about a stain on his new cloak. As he spoke, his fingernails extruded into long, curving claws.

'You cannot frighten me with your tricks,' Yaztromo said gruffly. He wished he felt as brave inside as his words sounded. He had no magic left, and a single sweep of those great talons would easily remove his head from his shoulders. 'In my time I have bested far worse creatures than you.'

'Perhaps, wizard, but I would hazard that you were younger then. Younger and stronger.' Cawlis shook his head, seemingly more in sorrow than in anger. As he did so, the skin peeled back, revealing tough, leathery flesh. A great crest of spines rose from his skull, erupting from his fast-retracting hair like volcanoes emerging from the sea. 'Pardon me. It does one good to assume one's true form from time to time, to remind oneself of one's real nature. Anyway, you have called me "monster"; why should I not look like one for our final confrontation?'

He stretched. Great ropes of muscle swelled along his arm. His shoulders broadened, tearing through his flimsy jerkin. Bone blossomed on his skin, flowed together, hardened into spiked armour. With a great creaking, his spine lengthened and his chest deepened. He stood taller now, even though he stooped and was hunched forward.

Yaztromo's heart skipped several beats as the Shapechanger reached down and plucked Dark-mane's recumbent form from the trampled grass. *Oh Chadda, where are you? I have need of your strong arm and fearless heart. I cannot sense your presence, yet I feel you are near. Hamaskis keep you alive, for all our sakes.*

'You know, wizard, when I was younger and considerably less civilized, I used to pull the arms off corpses and eat them. They were my favourite part of the meal, a real delicacy.' Cawlis's jaw had lengthened into a snout and his teeth had become savage, razor-edged fangs; but the quiet, urbane voice remained the same. How do they do that, Yaztromo remained enough of a scholar to wonder in annoyance; it would make it so much easier if they just snarled and wailed. 'It pains me to admit such things now but, well, you're not going to be telling anyone, are you? I promise I won't eat your arms; that would be too undignified for a mage of your reputation. Besides, how would you hold yourself up with no arm to grasp your old man's stick?'

The creature's boots were rent asunder and he gripped the ground with enormous five-toed claws. Mighty legs flexed automatically, the powerful muscles testing the pent-up power within them. He's only doing this to intimidate me, Yaztromo thought. He could have changed much quicker. He wants to impress me with his control And it's working, curse it!

'I do so feel that one must allow one's foes to keep their reputations intact. It may sound immodest, but it makes one's own triumphs look so much greater to posterity. Far better for my own

image that Darkmane be a mighty hero and you a great but age-diminished wizard. If the real truth were known — and I'm sorry to have to say this so bluntly — that you and he were a pair of lucky, incompetent blunderers, then I wouldn't look very good either, would I?'

The transformation was complete. A twisted giant stood before Yaztromo, clutching the body of his friend like a child's doll, and he himself stood before it, bereft of all power.

'Oh, do tell me, have you any spells left?' Cawlis asked conversationally.

It took all of Yaztromo's willpower to keep from freezing on the spot. *He knows*, he thought momentarily. *He knows and he's just been toying with me. Frantically he tried to tap the power of the Bloodstone, but it was denied him still. No, that can't be true, otherwise he would already have attacked. That's it, you old goat, that's it! He's holding back. There must be a reason.*

'Why don't you come forward and find out? Then the stone will be gone and all your creations will fall back into the filth from which you summoned them!'

Cawlis looked pleased. 'Ah, then you have deduced the connection between them and the Bloodstone. It is truly a pleasure to deal with such a perceptive mind. You would not believe what dealing with Trolls can do to one's conversational skills.'

Yaztromo caught the edge of sly mockery in Cawlis's voice. It was as if the shape-shifter had made him the butt of some secret joke. He bristled inside, his pride protesting. Hold on, hold on, he thought suddenly. What are we really dealing with here? No Shapechanger Yaztromo had ever encountered had shown more than a fraction of this creature's boasted sorcerous ability. No Shapechanger could have kept hunger at bay long enough to make such a speech. The speech itself had been a taunt, daring him to spot what should have been obvious all along. Cawlis was right; he was getting old – but that didn't mean he was losing all his faculties.

'You're no Shapechanger,' Yaztromo said, trying to keep the revelation as matter-of-fact as he was able.

'Very good, old man. I wondered how long it would take you to divine the truth. The real truth.'

Suddenly Yaztromo was very afraid indeed.

24

Master of Shadows

Darkmane ducked beneath the sweep of Axion's claw. Suddenly everything rippled. The mist was gone and they stood once more in Hellsgate Keep, but it was a Hellsgate Keep subtly altered. It looked newer, the stones were not yet eroded. Great banners fluttered from the towers, the noise of their flapping like a distant flock of birds. This was how it looked centuries ago, when it was the capital of Axion's secret empire, he realized.

Before him stood a young man, clad in outlandish garments, garments that belonged to another time. The man was as tall as Darkmane and just as strongly built, a warrior-king. His face was handsome, his brow high and intelligent. Sinister wisdom showed in his deep, black eyes.

'Now, Chadda Darkmane, you must learn what death feels like.' His five interwoven voices were still Axion's. He aimed a blow at Darkmane; it was clumsy and obvious, and the warrior should have been able to avoid it with ease. But his body felt slow and heavy, his reflexes dulled into shadows of their usual speed. He

knew that he was Axion's puppet. That here, in this
realm of mists and memory, the sorcerer was his master.

The blow crashed into his stomach and the pain
doubled him over. He managed to raise one arm to fend
off a blow to his head. Axion's fist connected with awful
force. Darkmane's arm went numb. The sorcerer brought
up a knee into his chest. A rib gave under the impact
and the warrior reeled away. He found himself at the
head of a flight of stairs, a bloody froth foaming on his
lips.

'This is as close as you normally come to death's all-
devouring realm, human; hurt but still functioning. Now
I will take you a stage further.'

A fist like a mace connected with Darkmane's jaw,
breaking it. He reeled backwards down the stairs. As he
fell, Axion kicked him, hard, increasing the speed of his
fall as he tumbled. Each step slammed into his wounded
side; lances of agony tore at his heart. He knew that
each impact was driving his fractured ribs further into his
lungs. Soon he would drown in his own blood.

He lay at the foot of the stairs, trying to force himself
to rise. There was a great roaring in his ears. His vision
contracted until he was staring down a long, dark tunnel.
Dimly he was aware of Axion standing over him. He
looked up into the gloating face of his enemy and realized that this was the one foe he could not overcome.

'Die!' Axion said and his fist descended, fracturing
Darkmane's skull. Consciousness fled from Darkmane's
shattered body.

On some dim, primordial level he was still aware of
what was happening. Time passed in seconds and in
years. He sensed his body bloat and putrefy, the very
nature of his flesh changing. His mind was dislocated

from his physical body by a mist. Darkmane fought back, pushing through the barriers that clouded his awareness. They gave way, and he was back inside his own decaying corpse. Chadda Darkmane opened his dead, worm-eaten eyes and rose to his feet once more, driven by his burning, indomitable will.

'Good,' Axion said simply. He was still young and strong, but his face was grave.

Darkmane saw the grey-green flesh begin to slough off his own hands and flexed his skeletal fingers. He no longer breathed. He lurched to his feet, staggering and flailing like a marionette with its strings cut. It occurred to him that the tables had been utterly turned. He was now in the position Axion had occupied when they had first met, trying to move a dead, undead body by force of will alone. He advanced on the sorcerer, clutching before him with bony fingers.

Axion gestured, and beams of light danced from his fingers – and Darkmane burned. Unimaginable agonies seared him. Darkmane knew this was no reprieve but a deeper and worse form of torture.

Axion pronounced a spell, and fountains of acid spurted at Darkmane's feet. Hissing and sizzling, he sank slowly into the pool. Despite having no nerves, he still felt pain. He wanted to scream, but his vocal cords had been eaten away. Axion spread his arms and called in a high-pitched screech. He was answered by a gathering shadow, which spiralled in the mist-white sky. Hordes of carrion birds descended and began to peck at Darkmane's corpse.

He fell forward into a sea of endless agony. When oblivion finally came, he welcomed Death as his oldest, dearest friend.

*

Shadowmaster

Darkmane was a spark falling through the velvet blackness of infinite night, dragged ever downward into the gravity well of an enormous black hole. Other sparks, of many different colours and shades, spun down round him. They were the souls of others, he knew at once, each making the last trip of their own personal life-journeys. Far below him, at the end of the drop, the souls touched the surface of that dark mass, sparkled and instantly were gone.

He was barely aware, his sense of self splintering away. This was death, he knew, final and forever. When he reached the end of that fall, it would all be over. His life was done, the end of his path reached. Acceptance swept through what was left of his consciousness.

He sensed another presence near by, a familiar one. It came alongside him and touched him through the darkness. It belonged to Axion, the taker of his life. He felt the mage's thoughts slide into his dulling mind.

I killed you, Darkmane. I am sorry. It was necessary for my freedom. Your death showed me the path, corrupted the very heart of the Bloodstone, introduced entropy to a place where it had never been. I could not kill myself but I could kill you. I have made you the vessel through which Death entered the unchanging realm in the heart of the jewel, the jewel of my heart. You have provided my way out.

Darkmane no longer cared. He just wanted to lose himself within the midnight oblivion that awaited him. To fade into that mass, to become one with all the other dead souls, to partake in the culmination of the universe.

No, Darkmane. You must go back. Your time is not yet and you have unfinished business among the living. Yaztromo needs you; Allansia needs you. The Demon, Cawlis, must be defeated. His existence, at least, I can help you undo. Let it be some small atonement for my sins.

Master of Shadows

White fire burned through Darkmane's consciousness. He rose slowly through an infinite void, gathering vapour-trails of memories about him as he ascended. They seemed strange to him; he saw old friends and enemies, their faces subtly distorted. He relived his training as a warrior and his induction as a warrior of Salamonis. Slowly he realized that the memories were his own, echoes floating through the Bloodstone's heart, echoes of his life.

His upward flight accelerated. He felt as light as a bird borne aloft on a current, fast as a mote of light. Feelings came flooding back, senses racing through his reborn body like a river breaching a dam. His reborn body breathed for the first time and the air was sweeter than nectar. Darkmane opened his eyes.

Cawlis stood above him, one claw raised to strike.

25

The Shape of Death

The Bloodstone blazed. Radiant energy surged through Yaztromo's mind. Knowledge flooded him, bursting the banks of his mind. Images flickered through his brain in a torrent. For an instant he and the Bloodstone were one.

He sensed Axion's departure from the stone, slipping out of this world and into the next. He saw the web of energy that linked the jewel both to the spells surrounding Hellsgate Keep and to all of Cawlis's creations. Axion had kept a final secret from the Shapechanger: that old spells linked the Bloodstone to the wells below the castle, and that its energies had infused the mutations with life. It was a secret that Yaztromo now knew, as if he had known it for ever.

Yaztromo peered into Cawlis's mind, and what he saw revolted him. Memories of flickering pits of sulphurous flame and darkened lands through which unholy Demons walked danced in his head. He saw the wretched thing that was Cawlis enter the world and take possession of the Shapechanger mage who had attempted to summon and bind him. That Shapechanger had known all the lore concerning Axion, the legendary creator of his race

The Shape of Death

Yaztromo was party to the full extent of the fiend's devious plans and nightmare ambitions.

Now that Axion was gone, the Bloodstone had become unstable. Without a spirit to restrain it, the forces holding it together were beginning to unravel. Great waves of power flowed through the old wizard as all the gem's energy threatened to discharge at once. His whole body blazed with the wild insanity of pure magic.

He struggled to focus and control what was happening. A lesser mage than Yaztromo might so easily have gone mad under the impact of that mind-shattering tide of mystical energy and stored memories. Yaztromo was pinned to the spot.

Cawlis's inhuman eyes widened as he saw what was happening. He let Darkmane fall and bounded towards the wizard, his great claws clutching for the fast-disintegrating Bloodstone.

Yaztromo knocked him aside with a glance of his eyes. A wave of white energy drove the Demon back across the glade. For a second he lay, sprawled in the dirt, then he picked himself up. He could still escape. Before the old man had mastered the Bloodstone's last discharge, he would be gone. With the jewel destroyed, he had no reason to stay. There would be plenty of further opportunities and time enough for revenge. This was a mere setback – not a final defeat.

He felt something tap him on the back.

'We have unfinished business, Demon,' said Darkmane, his mouth a thin line. 'Ever since Drystone, we have had unfinished business.'

'Then let us finish it,' said the Demon and lashed out with his claws.

Darkmane leapt to avoid Cawlis's attack. The blow was

swift, but his reborn body was swifter. His wounds had healed somehow, and he moved as surefootedly as a cat. Glancing about him, he glimpsed the bodies of his fallen companions. A black rage filled him.

'That is for Weasel,' he grated as his sword struck home. The blow should have decapitated Cawlis: the blade was driven with all the force of Darkmane's mighty arms; it could have felled an oak tree. But to Darkmane's horror, the blow flowed right through the shape-shifter's form; Cawlis's flesh knitted together behind it.

'I have grown stronger since our last meeting, little man, and more used to your world and its weapons. You cannot harm me now,' Cawlis mocked. Something of the Demon's ancient evil showed in his eyes; malevolent wisdom as old as time was written there. 'You consider yourself a mighty warrior? Test your prowess on one whose schooling in combat comes from a thousand years in the Pit!'

Cawlis's form altered once more, flowing into a newer, sleeker shape. Just looking at his pulsing, multi-hued form made Darkmane's eyes ache. The thing swept towards him, swift as the tide, fluid as quicksilver. A talon flashed across Darkmane's face. It was so sharp that for a few moments he did not realize he had been cut, until the warm blood flowed down his cheek and his face stung.

'It is always better to fight in one's true form. Better the devil you know, as it were, eh, human?'

Darkmane feinted a blow to the left then struck down at the Demon's leg, attempting to hamstring it. Once more his weapon passed harmlessly through the monster's flesh. Cawlis's counter-attack almost knocked Darkmane off his feet.

So began a nightmare game of cat and mouse. Realizing with despair that he could not hurt the Demon by physical strength, Darkmane fought defensively, hoping merely to stay alive long enough for a miracle to happen. The Demon seemed only too happy to toy with him, stalking him round the glade, occasionally cutting at him with a sweep of a talon or a lash from his new-grown tail.

Darkmane's limbs grew heavy with fatigue and his clothing became sodden with blood. He knew it would only be a matter of time before the Demon tired of this game and caught him. With every second he grew slower, his movements less co-ordinated, his swordsman-ship faltering. With every second the Demon grew more confident and malicious.

When the end came, it came quickly. Cawlis leapt forward. Reflexively, Darkmane stop-thrust with his long-sword, driving it through the Demon's chest and out through his back. The attack did not seem to hurt Cawlis at all. The Demon's claws gripped Darkmane's back, shredding his armour, and the warrior found himself in a crushing embrace. Cawlis's face was so close to his that he could smell the Demon's perfumed breath and look directly into his sardonic, glittering eyes.

'Now it is time to say farewell,' Cawlis said, his jaws moving in a leisurely way towards Darkmane's throat.

In his mind's eye, Yaztromo saw the mutant army collapse back into protoplasmic slime, the sinister ener-gies which had bound their forms together vanishing, along with the gem that had been their linchpin. He saw the vats bubble and overflow. He was in many places simultaneously, and he felt detached from them all.

He was dimly aware of Darkmane's protracted struggle with the Demon. He was as aware of it as he was of the great web of spells surrounding Hellsgate Keep. They were beautiful beyond belief, intricately wrought and far more demanding of his attention. If only he could memorize their pattern before they faded.

Wait! What was he thinking of? His mind had become temporarily unhinged by the sudden flow of power. There was something important which he had to do, and soon. Now what was it? Yes, defeat the Demon. He must defeat Cawlis!

Awareness flooded back into him. He stood in the forest glade once more, watching Cawlis's jaws widen round Darkmane's neck. It was like watching a snake's jaws distend to swallow an egg. Unhesitatingly, he marshalled the Bloodstone's fast-dissipating power. Yaztromo reached out with his mind and touched Darkmane's blade. White fire burned. The blade glowed sun-bright.

Screaming, Cawlis released Darkmane and fell to his knees. He had never known such agony, not even while enduring all the torments in the Pit. The mortal mage's spell hurt like nothing he had ever encountered.

Darkmane saw the Demon collapse, and he smelled the ozone stink of wild magic in the air. He reached forward and grasped the hilt of his sword. It felt hard and warm, and his hand tingled pleasurably at the contact. Darkmane saw Yaztromo's fingers being to move again. He no longer seemed rooted to the spot.

After the blade came free, Cawlis leapt to his feet and lashed out desperately — and Darkmane realized that the Demon had made a mistake. He parried the blow and was rewarded with the smell of scorching flesh. The Demon hissed in agony and turned to face the wizard. Yaztromo gestured. White lightning flickered across the rent air of the glade. The bolt sent Cawlis reeling and dancing across the ground, the grass beneath his feet bursting into flame.

Darkmane's next blow sheared a spine from the creature's shoulder. He reached out and tried to grab the warrior, but Darkmane was too quick. One long, talon-tipped hand was sliced cleanly off. Cawlis willed it to regrow, but nothing happened. Magics other than his were at work here now. He was fighting for his very life.

Fear made him redouble his efforts; he hit out wildly, willing a blow to strike home. Darkmane avoided his every effort; his counter-attacks fell swift and deadly as thunderbolts, nicking a limb here, shearing off a spine there. Cawlis stopped trying to dodge his blows and halted, panting.

'Stop toying with me,' he breathed. 'Finish it!'

Darkmane's blade burned into the Demon's chest. White fire pulsed through his brain. As consciousness fled, he made one last attempt to escape.

There was a huge burst of energy. Cawlis's twisted form began to writhe and split, as if he were being devoured from the inside by a horde of insects. Myriad small pieces of flesh began to transmute, becoming moths and flies and winged carrion-beetles. The cloud coalesced and drifted up like smoke.

'There is no escape, Demon,' Yaztromo pronounced. He gestured with his staff, sweeping it round in a great slow circle; it left a glowing trail in the air as it passed. A ball of pure magical power formed at its tip, the last remnants of the Bloodstone's fearsome strength. Yaztromo pointed the staff at the shimmering swarm of insects.

A hurricane of mystical power erupted, catching the tiny creatures as they flew. Each glowed briefly like a

firefly and then smouldered and burned until they were completely consumed in the fire. Specks of ash drifted down from the sky.

'The Demon is no more,' Yaztromo said simply.

Darkmane and Yaztromo stood in the silent glade, two survivors gazing at each other across a battlefield. Darkmane leaned on his sword. Yaztromo stood erect, his staff held like a victorious banner in one hand.

Darkmane gazed at the remains of Weasel and the corpse of the thing he had known as Star. He suddenly felt weary of violence and death and war. In the face of the carnage he had witnessed, Amonour seemed a hollow pursuit indeed.

His memory of the interior of the Bloodstone was fading just as one forgets the contents of a bad dream. Now he was not sure it had happened at all. But he knew he had changed. He would never again feel the same way about killing as before. And he could no longer make guiltless, superficial judgements about magic, about life and death. Things were more compli-cated than black or white, good or evil. All things were a mixture of the two. Weasel had been. Axion had been. Star had been. Even Cawlis had faced his end with a certain dignity.

'What now?' Yaztromo asked softly.

'I must find a quiet place to think, old man.'

The wizard smiled. He had expected some declaration of triumph, some boastful speech about how it had all been done for Amonour. 'You're learning, Chadda Dark-mane. You're learning.'

The wizard gave a high-pitched whistle, and his pet flapped down from a nearby tree to rest upon his shoulder. 'Come. Our paths run together for a while longer.'

Steve Jackson's
SORCERY!

1. *The Shamutanti Hills*
Your search for the legendary Crown of Kings take you to the Shamutanti Hills. Alive with evil creatures, lawless wanderers and bloodthirsty monsters, the land is riddled with tricks and traps waiting for the unwary traveller. Will you be able to cross the hills safely and proceed to the second part of the adventurer – or will you perish in the attempt?

2. *Kharé – Cityport of Traps*
As a warrior relying on force of arms, or a wizard trained in magic, you must brave the terror of a city built to trap the unwary. You will need all your wits about you to survive the unimaginable horrors ahead and to make sense of the clues which may lead to your success – or to your doom!

3. *The Seven Serpents*
Seven deadly and magical serpents speed ahead of you to warn the evil Archmage of your coming. Will you be able to catch them before they get there?

4. *The Crown of Kings*
At the end of your long trek, you face the unknown terrors of the Mamang Fortress. Hidden inside the keep is the Crown of Kings – the ultimate goal of the *Sorcery!* epic. But beware! For if you have not defeated the Seven Serpents your arrival has been anticipated . . .

Complete with all the magical spells you
will need, each book can be played either
on its own or as part of the whole epic.

DUNGEONEER
Marc Gascoigne and Pete Tamlyn

Now you and your friends can create your own fantasy movies! Imagine that you are the director and your friends are the cast of heroes. Will you send them to battle with the evil wizard or recover the Dragons' hoard? The choice is yours, and *Dungeoneer* makes the exciting world of fantasy role-playing accessible in a thoroughly user-friendly manner.

BLACKSAND!
Marc Gascoigne and Pete Tamlyn

Sprawling like the corpse of some giant creature, Port Blacksand is a festering den of pirates and brigands. Unforeseen dangers lurk around every street corner and in every dark alleyway. Devious plots and crimes are hatched in every tavern. Thieves and assassins slip through the shadows. Ancient mysteries lurk in the cellars and sewers. But the infamous City of Thieves is also home to excitement and adventure beyond compare!

The second volume in the Advanced Fighting Fantasy series which started with *Dungeoneer*.